Metal Clay 101 for Beaders

Metal Clay 101 for Beaders

CREATE CUSTOM FINDINGS, BEADS, EMBELLISHMENTS & CHARMS

Kristal Wick, 1960

An Imprint of Sterling Publishing
387 Park Avenue South
New York, NY 10016

ISBN 978-1-4547-0759-2

Library of Congress Cataloging-in-Publication Data

Wick, Kristal, 1960-
Metal clay 101 for beaders / Kristal Wick.
pages cm
Includes index.
ISBN 978-1-4547-0759-2 (pbk.)
1. Beadwork. 2. Beads. 3. Precious metal clay. 4. Jewelry making.
I. Title. II. Title: Metal clay one hundred one for beaders.
TT860.W5886 2013
746.5--dc23
2013002070

Distributed in Canada by Sterling Publishing
c/o Canadian Manda Group, 165 Dufferin Street
Toronto, Ontario, Canada M6K 3H6
Distributed in the United Kingdom by GMC Distribution Services
Castle Place, 166 High Street, Lewes, East Sussex, England BN7 1XU
Distributed in Australia by Capricorn Link (Australia) Pty. Ltd.
P.O. Box 704, Windsor, NSW 2756, Australia

For information about custom editions, special sales, and premium and corporate purchases, please contact Sterling Special Sales at 800-805-5489 or specialsales@sterlingpublishing.com.

Email academic@larkbooks.com for information about desk and examination copies. The complete policy can be found at larkcrafts.com.

Manufactured in China

2 4 6 8 10 9 7 5 3 1

larkcrafts.com

contents

38

44

60

63

80

82

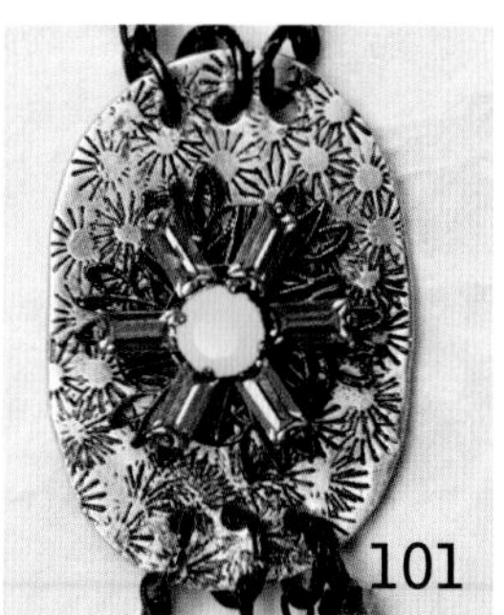
101

106

46
50
54
57
66
69
72
76
86
89
92
95
112
115
118

introduction

BEADERS & JEWELRY MAKERS, meet your new BFF (Best Friend Forever)—Metal Clay!

Everyone who knows me, knows I'm a beadaholic, but I'm also addicted to metal clay. My foray into the world of clay actually began with an obsession with raku. I was in awe of the surprising results that transpired from the mystical combination of fire, glazes, garbage cans, and dried cow manure! Metal clay has more predictable results and a much less involved firing process (no dried cow manure!), but the thrill of starting with a lump of squishy stuff and ending up with spectacular metal jewelry can't be topped. Breathtaking and extremely soul satisfying, metal clay has me hooked. I got the bug in my very first beginning class at a big bead convention and haven't stopped.

Combining my love affair with beads, Swarovski crystals, and pearls with the introduction of copper and bronze metal clay to the silver clay world, I simply *had* to make my own findings. You know the thrill of finishing up a seed bead masterpiece and searching for the perfect finding, toggle, or clasp and asking, "Why doesn't this come in copper or a vintage-looking patina finish?" (the kind that looks like you dug it up in your grandma's back yard)? Well, search no more my beady peeps! *Metal Clay 101 for Beaders* shows you simple techniques and projects to make with endless variations. There are many books out there on metal clay, but I wanted to make one especially for beadaholics (myself included)! My goal is not only to teach you how to make the projects featured here but

also to light the fire of inspiration and boost your confidence for exploring the world of metal clay and creating the perfect union of beads and metal clay. If you've never played with clay before, now is the time! You'll be thrilled by how easily you can customize your findings and create one-of-a-kind metal clay beads to enhance your jewelry.

Whether you enjoy the look of bronze, copper, silver or all three, you'll learn techniques for each clay type along with a variety of patterned finishes. From pet tags to earrings; birdhouse pendants to cupcakes; end cones to magnetic clasps, you'll discover a whole new world of making exactly what you want for *your* jewelry style whether you sell it, give it to your friends, or simply wear it yourself. Play with patinas, texture plates, stampings, and resin for some interesting and unusual effects. I'll show you step by step how to make each project, all the materials you'll need, and the techniques to assure your success!

So thumb through the projects, peruse the Idea Book starting on page 122 for even more inspiration, pick out your first project, and jump in—the clay is fine!

The Basics

Metal Clay

Metal Clay Types

Metal clays are sold in paper-thin sheets, as a powder, in pre-filled syringes, in jars as slip (thin, watered-down clay), and in packages of lump clay. I used lump clay for all the projects in this book. PMC (Precious Metal Clay), PMC Pro, PMC+, 22-karat gold clay, Quick-fire Steel, Quick-fire White, and Art Clay Silver are a few of the different types of clays on the market. Explore the wide variety, but keep in mind that each type must be kept and stored separately.

Sintering

Sintering is the heating process that causes metal particles to become a coherent mass, and it occurs just before the metal reaches its melting temperature. Sintering is how clay molecules become solid when fired. Metal clay is composed of tiny metal particles, an organic binder, and water. You'll form metal clay into the desired shapes, and once it's completely dry (often referred to as bone dry), you'll fire your pieces in a kiln or with a torch. Such an intense heat vaporizes the binder and water and leaves only solid, fully sintered metal pieces. That's why metal clay shrinks.

My Favorite Metal Clays

When I find a product that makes me happy, I tend to stick with it. I used PMC Sterling Silver, PMC3, BRONZclay, Fastfire BRONZclay, and COPPRclay for all the projects in this book, and I have been pleased with their consistency and final results.

PMC Sterling

Sterling silver clay is three times stronger than fine silver clay, and it has a longer working time than all the other silver clays. The only downside I've experienced with PMC Sterling is that it requires two firings, and the second firing must be in a kiln.

Metal Content	92.5% fine silver, 7.5% copper
Fired Product	0.925 (sterling) silver
Shrinkage	15–20%

PMC3

This product runs neck and neck with PMC Sterling as my fave silver clay. PMC3 consists of 85 percent fine silver and 15 percent binder. You can embed and fire some natural gemstones, cubic zirconia, dichroic glass, and porcelain into the clay as long as the embedded object can withstand the firing temperature. PMC3 stays workable longer than other PMC silver clays, with the exception of PMC Sterling.

Product Content	85% fine silver, 15% binder
Fired Product	0.999 (fine) silver
Shrinkage	12–15%

Metal clay types

BRONZclay

BRONZclay was the first base metal available as a clay. It's much more affordable than silver clay, but requires a more complex firing procedure. Bronze clay pieces must be buried in activated carbon inside a stainless steel container before going in the kiln. Torch firing is not an option.

Product Content	89% copper, 11% tin, water, binder
Fired Product	bronze, 90% density of cast bronze
Shrinkage	20%

Fastfire BRONZclay

Fastfire BRONZclay fires much faster than regular BRONZclay, and I have not noticed any difference in the end result if the clay is fired properly.

Product Content	90% copper, 10% tin, water, binder
Fired Product	bronze, 90% density of cast bronze
Shrinkage	5–10%

COPPRclay

Copper clay is much more affordable than her silver sister. Copper is fun to work with, and you can even throw it on a potter's wheel to create larger pieces. You can enamel, patina, guild, and carve copper clay. The rich color of copper and bronze is very fashion-forward and popular.

Product Content	pure copper, water, binder
Fired Product	pure copper
Shrinkage	approximately 20%

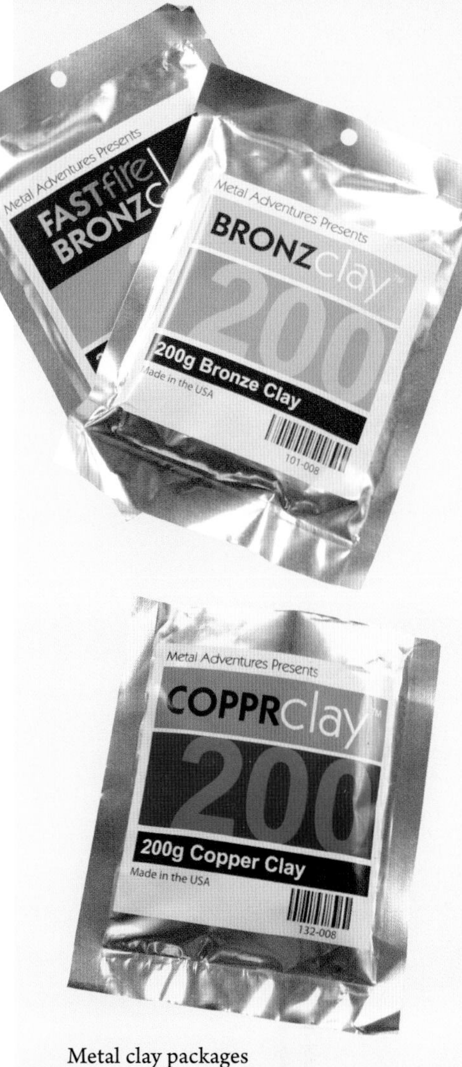

Metal clay packages

SLIP

Slip is simply watered-down metal clay. You can purchase small containers of slip or make your own. To make slip, start by chopping dried clay into little bits (photo A) or grinding it in a dedicated coffee bean grinder. Then, as shown in photo B, moosh distilled water into the ground clay with a small palette knife using a motion that is similar to icing a cake. The ideal slip is the consistency of icing. Transfer your slip to a small container with a tight-sealing lid (photo C), and add all your dried or wet clay scraps to this container. Finally, I suggest writing the type of clay on the lid of the slip container with a permanent marker ... you'll thank me later!

A

B

C

Metal Clay Tools and Materials

You can use the same roller, work surface, and texture templates for different metal clays as long as you thoroughly wash these tools after using them. You must have a separate file set for sanding silver clay, and keep these files away from bronze or copper clay. Discoloration and contamination can occur if dust or tiny bits of different clays mingle.

Kiln

There are quite a few kilns on the market these days, and knowing which kiln to purchase can be a bit confusing. There is an abundance of detailed information on tabletop kilns on the Internet. Solid Web research will help you decide which kiln will be best for you. Also, I suggest creating a few metal clay pieces and firing your first few batches at a local bead store or paint-your-own-pottery studio. Many of these shops will fire a small kiln load for a fee. If they do, ask the shop owner if you can watch her load and fire your pieces.

The only "must" for a tabletop jewelry kiln is that it be programmable. You'll set the temperatures and hold times, turn on the kiln, and walk away. Make certain to fire the kiln away from anything flammable, and always allow 5 to 7 feet (1.5 to 2.1 m) of safe space around the kiln. I fire outside on my patio or on a concrete floor in my basement.

A *thermocouple* is a device for measuring temperature and a very important element of a kiln. Use a damp paper towel to frequently clean your thermocouple, and make sure it is always in the right place—about ½ inch (1.3 cm) of the tip should extend inside the kiln. Take care not to bump the thermocouple out of place—this will cause a firing to be unsuccessful.

Do not place anything on the floor of the kiln. Always place your metal clay pieces or your steel container on top of a kiln shelf or board to ensure even heating.

After you fire a stainless steel container, black flecks will be left inside the kiln. These are easily removed by carefully vacuuming with a small brush or nozzle attachment. The flecks won't hurt the kiln, but you will want to regularly vacuum inside and around the kiln to keep it free of dust and debris.

Kiln

Inside of kiln

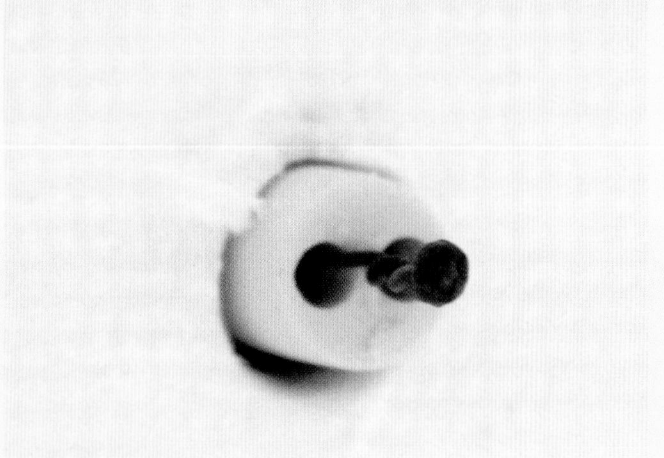

Thermocouple

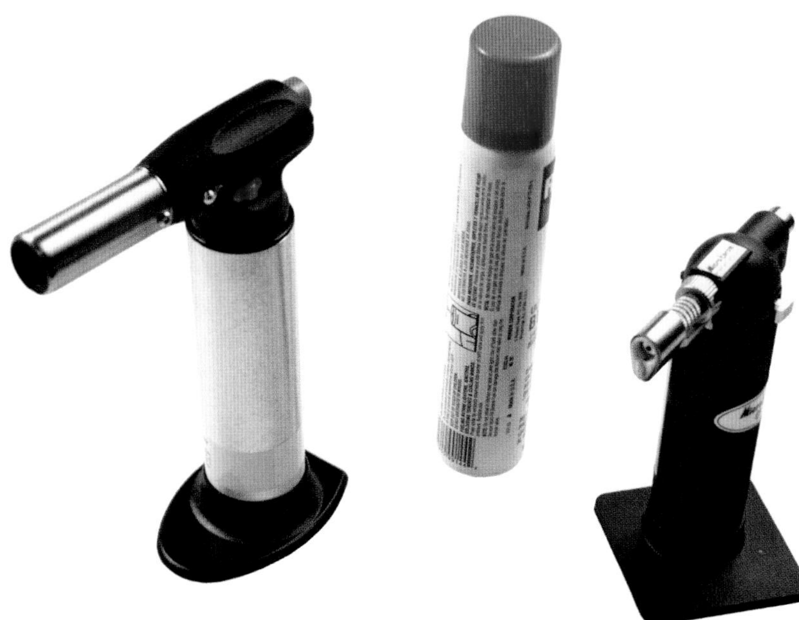

Butane torches and fuel

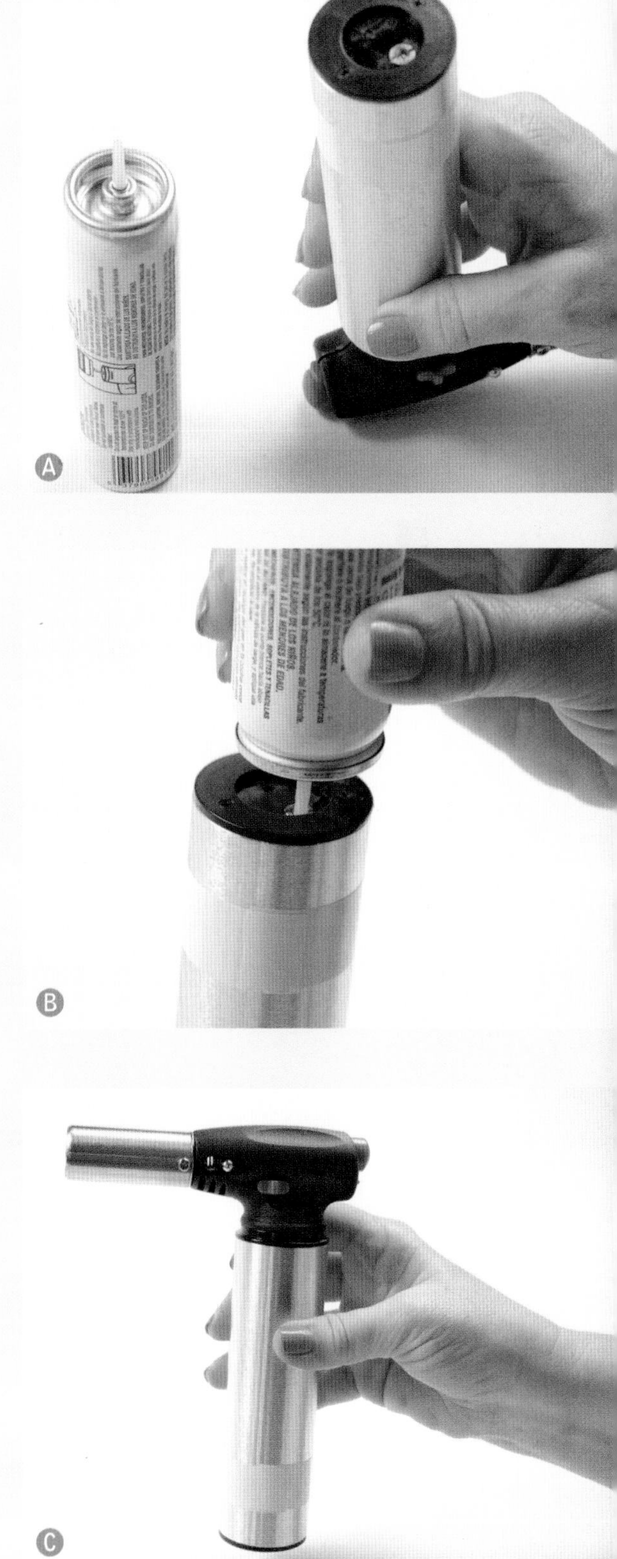

Torch

I recommend firing all metal clay in a kiln for the most successful results and consistency. However, there will be times you may want to fire more quickly. If so, use a butane torch or a crème brûlée torch to fire small silver clay pieces.

Filling a Butane Torch

When you purchase a torch, it does not come filled with butane. So, that's your first step, and it's not as scary as you think ... really! But, just to be safe, I always fill my torch outside. Here's how to do it:

1. Take off the butane cap, and hold the torch upside down (photo A).

2. Push the tip of the butane canister into the filling hole on the bottom of the torch (photo B). Firmly press the can, and you will hear the torch filling up with butane. It only takes a few seconds, and you can tell the torch is full when you hear a spitting noise.

3. Remove the butane canister, set the torch upright, and let it sit for a minute or so (photo C). You're now ready for some flaming!

METAL CLAY TOOLBOX

- Metal Clay, 100-gram package
- Nonstick work surface
- Rubber block or hockey puck
- Distilled water
- Olive oil
- Spray Oil
- Metal clay conditioner and release agent
- Silicone rubber bowls
- Sealable plastic bags and plastic wrap
- Glass jars
- Plastic slats or playing cards
- Roller
- Snake roller
- Small paintbrushes
- Toothpicks
- Slicing blade
- Craft knife
- Clay-shaping tools
- Texture plates
- Armatures
- Coffee mug warmer
- Needle files
- Tweezers
- Fiber brick
- Kiln
- Activated coconut carbon
- Firing container
- Brass brushes
- Tumbler and shot

Acrylic rollers, playing cards, plastic slats, self-healing mat

Metal Clay Toolbox

Here's a list of every material and tool you must have to get started working with metal clay. I've arranged them in order of use—work surfaces; liquids and lubricants; containers and storage; sculpting aids; drying and firing; and finishing and polishing.

Nonstick Work Surface

A self-healing quilter's mat, thick plastic bags, or nonstick plastic sheets are perfect work surfaces.

Rubber Block or Hockey Puck

Use a rubber block or a hockey puck for a work surface when creating small pieces you may not be able to pick up or hold. I strongly suggest buying a new, inexpensive hockey puck. (Do not, under any circumstances, use the one from your hubby's collection—you know, the one with a signature on it!)

Distilled Water

I suggest using only distilled water when working with metal clay. Keep a jug in your studio, and fill up a spray bottle or pour some out in a small bowl when needed. There can be some funky stuff in your tap water—better to be cautious and keep it clean.

Olive Oil

Use olive oil sparingly to lubricate your hands and other surfaces that may stick to the clay. (I always rub in a dab or two on my cuticles—why not multitask and have a spa/clay day all in one?) Thoroughly wash the oil off all surfaces at the end of your work time. Some types of rubber and other surfaces will deteriorate if olive oil is left on too long.

Spray Oil

An aerosol spray oil is handy for oiling texture plates because the lubricant gets into every nook and cranny. Make certain to thoroughly wash the texture plates after use.

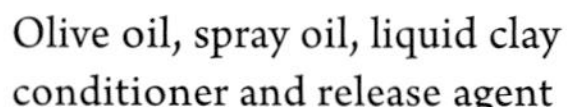

Olive oil, spray oil, liquid clay conditioner and release agent

Metal Clay Conditioner and Release Agent

I really love Slik, a natural, silky balm made out of soy, almond, and aloe. I use it to condition my clay and to keep it moist and workable longer. (For more details, see Conditioning the Clay on page 20.)

Silicone Rubber Bowls

I use silicone rubber sauce bowls for water dishes (and for sorting beads and other small treasures!). These bowls come in handy for so many uses you'll wonder how you ever lived without them.

Sealable Plastic Bags and Plastic Wrap

Always double wrap your working clay quickly to prevent it from drying out, and then place the wrapped clay in a sealable plastic bag.

Glass Jars

Use small, lidded glass jars, such as those used for baby food, to make a mini clay solarium and keep your clay hydrated.

Plastic Slats or Playing Cards

I like to use both of these tools for measuring the thickness of metal clay. The graduated slats are color-coded to indicate thickness. I use a permanent marker to write the thickness on each slat as well.

Roller

Clear acrylic rollers and plastic pipe both work well for evenly rolling out clay. Always spray a release agent or rub a dab of oil on the roller to prevent sticking.

Snake Roller

I like using the clear acrylic roller that has a handle on top for ease of movement. Here's how to use it:

1. Roll out a snake by hand (photo A).
2. Place the acrylic roller on top of the clay, and reroll it to create a perfectly even snake (photo B).

This tool also comes in handy for making clay balls the same size. Here's how to do it:

1. Roll out a snake. Place a ruler along the snake's edge.
2. Cut off precise lengths of clay, and roll these lengths into balls. Each ball will be exactly the same size and have the same amount of clay (photo C).

Clay conditioners and lotions

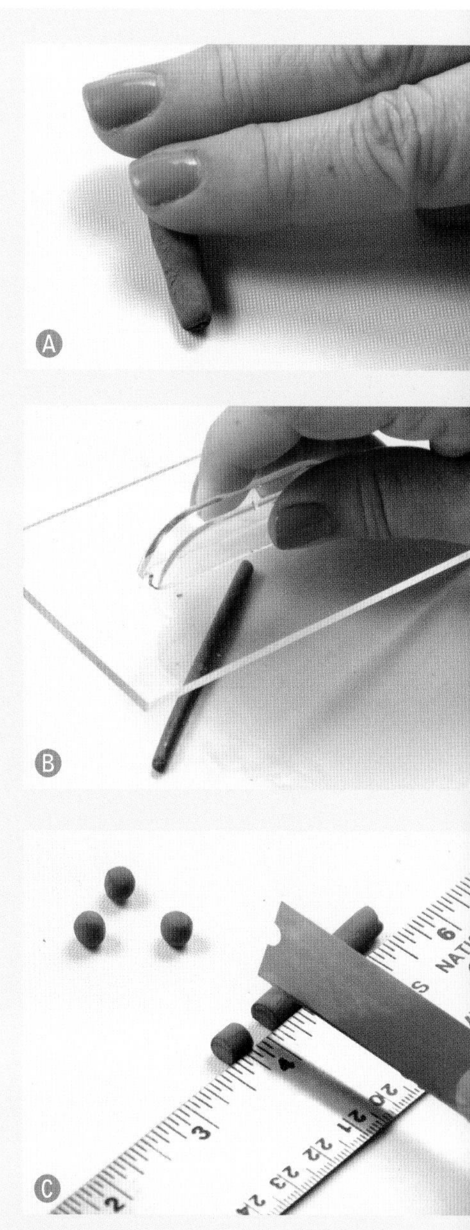

Plastic wrap, glass jar with lid, silicone rubber bowls, plastic bags

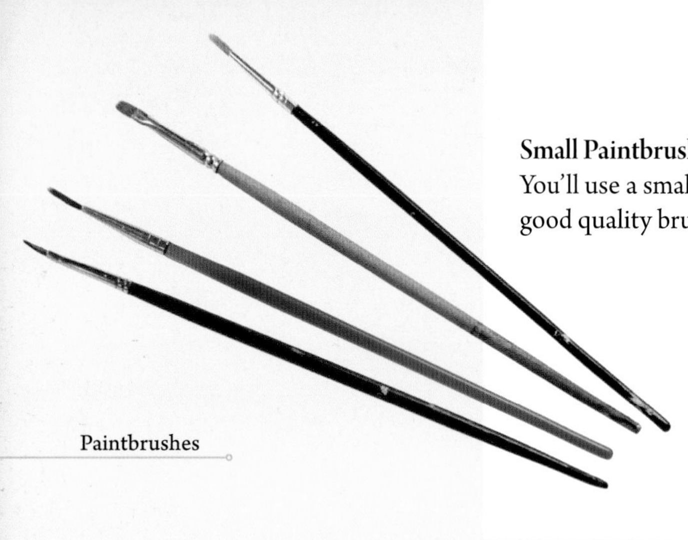

Paintbrushes

Small Paintbrushes

You'll use a small paintbrush for smoothing out cracks and applying slip. Purchase a good quality brush—cheaper ones can shed their bristles and be frustrating to use.

Toothpicks

Both pointed and flat toothpicks are useful. They're particularly handy for poking the clay and moving it around.

Slicing Blade

A slicing blade does not have a sharp tip at one end, but rather a cutting blade that runs the full length of one edge of the tool. Some slicing blades are rigid, some are flexible so you can cut curved lines and shapes, and some have serrated edges for making fun, decorative cuts.

Slicing blades, palette knife, craft knife, toothpicks

Craft Knife

I love making holes in dry metal clay with this tool. Here's how to do it:

1. Once a piece of clay is completely dry, place the pointed tip of a craft knife where you want the hole. Twirl the point around until the blade is all the way through the clay.

2. Flip over the metal clay piece, and repeat step 1 from the back of the clay to open the hole all the way through the piece.

Clay-Shaping Tools

A clay-shaping tool helps you push and prod tiny areas of clay into the desired form. Tool ends can be shaped like small palette knives, spheres, and needles—whatever it takes to get the job done.

Drilling a hole in the clay with a craft knife

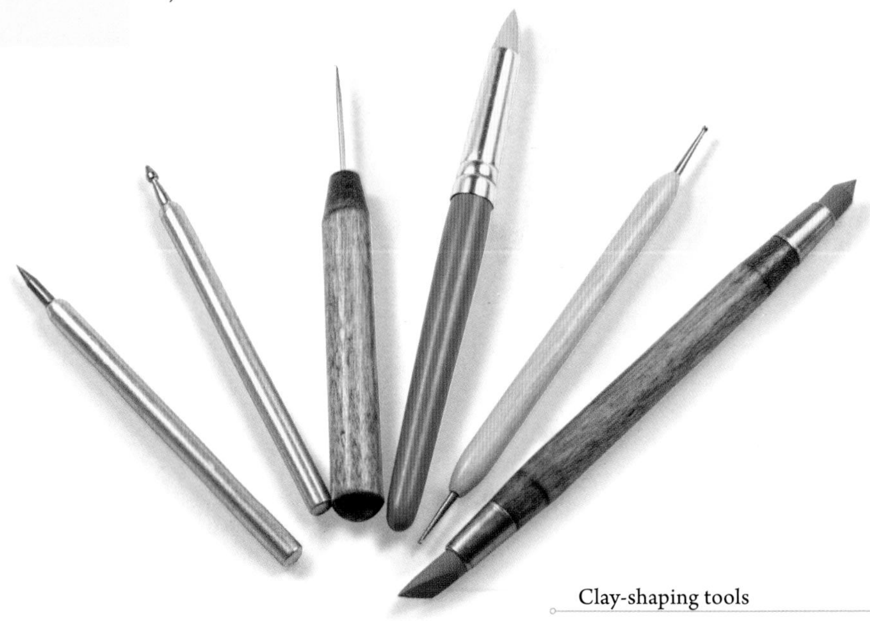

Clay-shaping tools

Texture Plates

Many great texture plates are made specifically for use with clay, but if you keep your eyes open, you'll find plenty of unique, alternative surfaces. Be sure to visit the cake-making department and rubber stamp aisles in your local craft store for interesting candy molds and other texture ideas.

Texture plates

Armatures

Armatures are internal cores, and there are two types to use when working with metal clay. One type of armature is burnable, and you will need to remove it after firing the clay. Examples of this type are cork clay, wood, paper clay, and puffed wheat or "O"-shaped breakfast cereal. The second type of armature remains as the foundation of the clay and is not removed. Hollow bisque beads are an example of this type of armature.

Armatures allow you to create hollow pieces that use much less clay. You can make armatures in any shape you wish. Once an armature is ready, you'll cover it with clay and fire. The base must always have a hole in it. The hole can be patched and re-fired after the core has been burned away.

Armatures

Coffee Mug Warmer

Dig way back in the darkest recesses of your cupboards or scour garage sales and thrift stores for an old-fashioned mug warmer, and dust it off. I keep a couple of these going at once to dry my clay pieces.

Coffee mug warmer for drying metal clay

Bisque beads

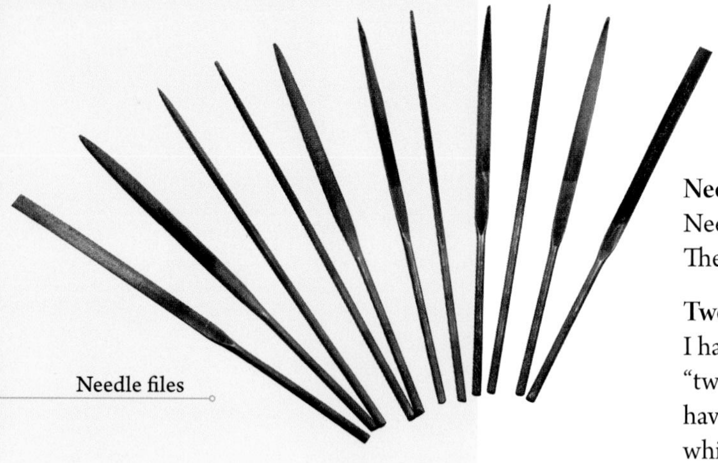

Needle files

Tweezers

Fiber brick

Brass brushes

Needle Files

Needle files come in handy to smooth out small interior crevices. The smaller the files, the better they'll serve you.

Tweezers

I have so many different tweezers, I'm proud to officially be labeled a "tweezers hoarder." Flat, sharp, round, small, paddle-shaped—I even have some with an interior light for better viewing! You'll find out which types you'll need rather quickly.

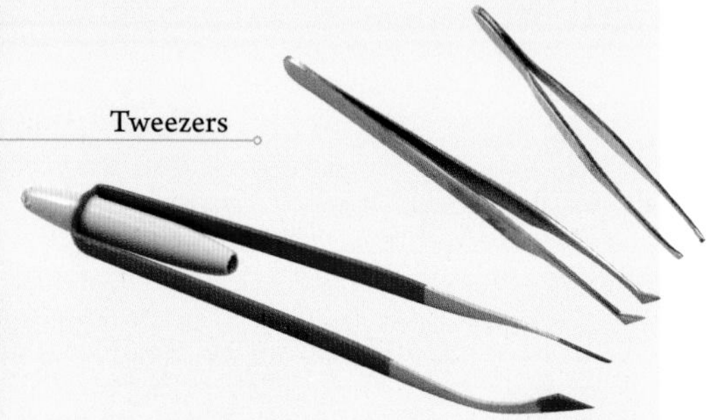

Fiber Brick

A fiber brick is made from compressed vermiculite and is heat resistant to 2400°F (1316°C). It is a great work surface for torch firing, and you can place hot pieces on it to cool. Purchase fiber bricks online or at a ceramic supply shop.

Brass Brushes

Use brass brushes for hand-polishing small areas of fired metal clay. Use one brush for silver and another for copper and bronze.

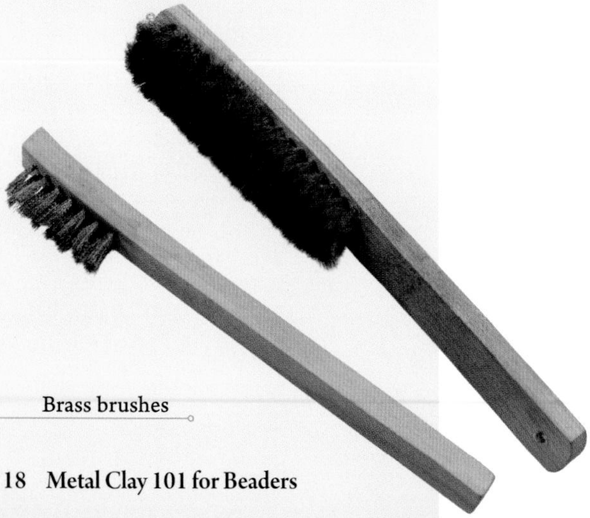

Tumbler and Shot

A rotary tumbler is one of the best purchases you'll make (besides your kiln). Tumbling pieces will give them a beautiful shine and harden the metal at the same time. Use 1 pound (0.45 kg) of rust-proof stainless steel shot in your tumbler. Add your jewelry pieces, a squirt of dish soap, and fill with water until it is 1 inch (2.5 cm) above the shot. Tumble until you're pleased with the shine, and then rinse and dry the metal. All shot is not created equal. Use shot that has a variety of shapes and sizes so it can shine every nook and cranny of the metal.

Tumbler and shot

Metal Clay Fundamentals

Working with metal clay is similar to playing with dough clay in grade school, but with a much better outcome! There are subtle differences between the different metal clays—some dry out faster than others; some are a bit grainier or smoother—but generally they are all delightful and easy to work with. Once fired, metal clay can be sawed, hammered, textured, drilled, patinated, or soldered.

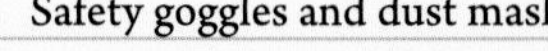

Safety goggles and dust mask

Safety

First things first: Let's talk about safety. Here are two very important safety practices you must always obey:

1. Whenever you're working with a substance that is fine enough to become airborne, wear a dust mask. Whether you're sifting carbon or sanding a bone-dry piece of metal clay, wear a mask!

2. Don't touch anything hot with your bare hands. Blisters never match your jewelry, so take great care and wear protective gloves when working with anything hot from the kiln or torch.

Storing Metal Clay

Metal clay keeps well in the refrigerator, but if possible I always try to use up an entire package at one sitting. Refrigerate your metal clay when you are not using it. Once a package has been opened, tightly wrap the remaining clay in plastic wrap and place it in a plastic bag that can be completely sealed.

Creating a Clay Solarium

Here is a simple method you can try to keep your clay moist:

1. Dab some olive oil, spray a bit of cooking oil, or rub Slik balm on your hands to keep the clay from sticking. Also, rub some oil on your work surface and any other tools you may use. Important: Don't use too much oil or you'll alter the makeup of the clay.

2. Place a damp paper towel in a small, lidded jar.

3. Open the clay package, and place the fresh clay on a piece of plastic wrap. Pinch off a quarter-sized piece of clay, and set it aside on an additional piece of plastic wrap to condition.

4. Tightly wrap the rest of the clay in plastic, place it in the jar, and firmly close the lid. This creates a little solarium to keep the clay moist. Keep your working clay (the small piece pinched off from the main clay) wrapped in a separate piece of plastic.

Conditioning Clay

You need to condition your metal clay right off the bat. Condition small lumps at a time to keep them moist and malleable.

1. Place a small amount of metal clay on plastic wrap.
2. Add a few drops of distilled water or a dab of Slik to the clay.
3. Fold the clay on top of itself. Fold the plastic wrap over the clay. The clay should be sandwiched between two layers of plastic.
4. Use a roller to roll the clay very thin and flat. Open the plastic wrap, fold the clay over itself again, and roll. Repeat this process a few times.
5. Let the clay rest in the plastic wrap for five minutes, and you're ready to go!

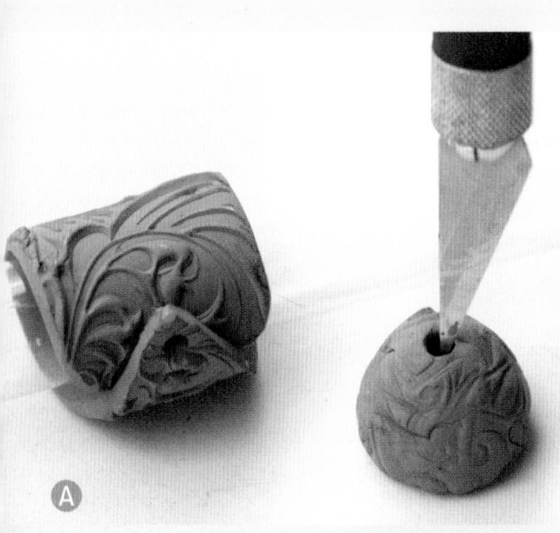

A

Sculpting Tips

Make sure to have a small cup of distilled water available, and add a drop or two as needed if the clay starts to dry out.

As you shape and mold the clay, bear in mind that it will shrink when fired. Make all pieces larger than your desired end result.

When creating metal clay elements for beading projects, make certain all of the metal edges are smooth so they don't cut the beading wire.

After boring holes with a craft knife (photo A), make sure to smooth the edges inside the hole. Use a thin paintbrush with a dab of water to soften any rough edges around and inside the holes.

Textures & How to Get Them

You can simply wander through your home and find all kinds of lovely surfaces you can use to texture clay. Examples of readily available items include lace, tree bark, silverware, rubber bath mats, and even the soles of rubber shoes and sandals. Just be sure to apply a spray release to every surface before pressing the clay into them.

B

Texture Plates

There are many wonderful texture plates (photo B), rubber stamps, and stencils perfect for pressing into metal clay. Keep in mind the desired size of your finished piece, and make sure the texture on the plate or stamp is small enough to render the whole effect on your completed piece. Frequently, large images get cut off and don't work well for jewelry. Always apply a spray release to the texture plates before pressing clay into them.

Texture & Thickness

Here is a simple way to roll out clay on a texture plate that results in a uniform clay thickness. If you want the textured clay to be 4 cards thick, first roll out a piece of clay 6 cards thick. Place this clay on top of the texture plate. Position 4 cards or plastic slats on each side of the texture plate next to the clay. Roll out the clay, carefully remove it from the plate, and you're ready to go.

Hammering Textures
After the metal clay pieces are fired and polished, you can use a chasing hammer to pound patterns into the metal surface (photo C). Silver metal clays are relatively soft and easy to hammer. Copper and bronze clays are harder, but can still be hammered.

Making Molds

Making your own molds is fun and much easier than you may think. Also, it is highly addictive! Some of the best molds are made from vintage buttons, silverware handles, and nature's beautiful leaves, pinecones, tree bark, and seashells. I suggest using two-part silicon cold-molding compound that dries in five minutes.

1. Knead equal amounts of the two-part silicon together until the compound is one solid color.
2. Roll the compound into a ball. Slightly press one side of the ball to flatten.
3. Press the desired object into the compound, and leave it in place for five minutes.
4. Pop the object out of the mold, and it's ready to use.

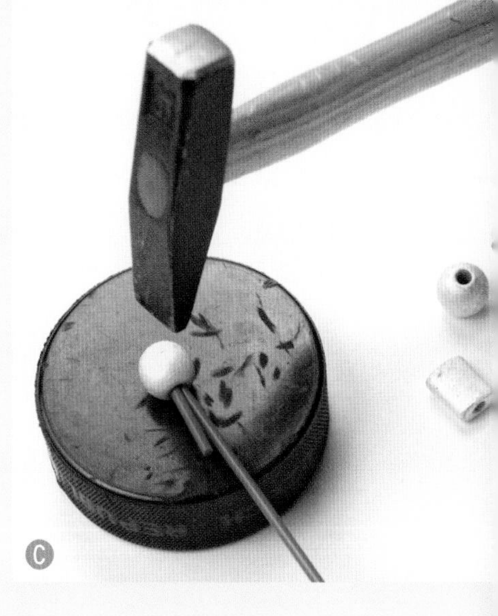
C

NOTE

When you press metal clay into a mold, let the clay dry completely before removing it.

Using Bisque Clay Bead Armatures

You can purchase ready-made bisque beads, coat them with metal clay slip, fire, and—voilà—half the weight and cost of solid beads, and consistently shaped beads every time! Bisque clay beads are sold in many different shapes and sizes. To make a handle to hold while coating bisque beads with clay, fold the end of a coffee stir straw in half, tuck it into the bisque bead, and make sure it's a tight fit (photo D). Water down the clay until it has a cream-like consistency, or use slip or syringe clay for this process.

D

Use a paintbrush to apply a light and even coat of thin clay to each bisque bead. Let the coat dry completely. Repeat this process to apply a total of six to eight coats of clay. Carefully remove the straw from the bead. Using the same process, apply six to eight coats of clay to the interior rim of each bead hole.

Fire the piece as usual.

If you want to place the fired beads in a tumbler, thread a pipe cleaner through the bead holes and loosely twist the ends together. (You don't want the pipe cleaner tight across the beads.) This keeps the shot from getting into the bead holes and becoming darn near impossible to remove!

Firing Metal Clay

Every package of metal clay includes firing instructions provided by the manufacturer. Here, you'll find the recommended time and temperature schedule to use when firing that particular clay. Note that the minimum firing times and temperatures are listed—this does not mean the clay will be totally sintered and strong. For example, PMC silver clay (not Sterling) achieves maximum strength only when kiln-fired at 1650°F (889°C) for two hours. Period. End of conversation. (Believe me, this immediate-gratification-oriented beader loves anything that can be fired in a few minutes.) I know... I know. "They" say you can fire PMC with a torch, and technically you can, but to be on the safe side I've made it a policy to fire a kiln load for two hours whenever possible. Since I never know where my jewelry will end up, it's much better to know every piece is fully sintered.

Kiln

You must always be certain that each piece of clay is completely dry before firing, or it will explode in the kiln. (You think I'm kidding?) Let the clay air dry or use a coffee mug warmer to speed up the process. Once a piece of clay is completely dry, it is referred to as *leather hard*. In this state, clay can be drilled, carved, or attached to similar pieces with slip. I recommend keeping a firing notebook so you can learn from your history. Notate all your observations—the successes and the boo-boos. (We all have them!) Your skills will grow with every experience.

Firing Containers

Many metal clay kits include the special container required for firing alloys. If you need to purchase a container separately, try a metal clay supplier or a restaurant supply store. Only use stainless steel or ceramic containers for firing PMC Sterling, BRONZclay, Fastfire BRONZclay, and COPPRclay. Never use aluminum containers.

Stainless steel firing container

When activating the carbon, leave the lid off the container. When firing metal clay in the carbon, keep the lid ajar so some oxygen can reach the pieces. With each firing, stainless steel pans will oxidize, turn dark, and shed black flakes. Simply vacuum the flakes after each firing. The flakes do not affect your kiln or firings, although they're messy little buggers and can end up everywhere, like glitter—only not as pretty.

Filling a Firing Container

Fill the bottom of the container with ½ to 1 inch (1.3 to 2.5 cm) of activated carbon. Place your clay pieces on top of the carbon, leaving ½ inch (1.3 cm) between them. Add 1 inch (2.5 cm) of carbon on top of the first layer, and position more clay pieces. Continue this process until the container is fully loaded, and then put on the lid. It's best to fire no more than 100 grams of metal clay at a time. Do not place any pieces within 1 inch (2.5 cm) of the kiln door if possible, or only place very thin pieces there. This tends to be the coolest area in a kiln, and it may not reach the target temperature during firing.

Activating Carbon

The carbon used to fill the container will need to be activated before firing metal clay. Activated carbon is good for approximately 100 to 125 hours of firing. Coconut shell-based carbon, coal-based carbon, and Magic Carbon all work differently with little consistency, so try them out before deciding which one you like best. Magic Carbon can give BRONZclay and Fastfire BRONZclay a patina or rainbow effect, but only some of the time. When a patina does occur, it's as thrilling as firing raku pottery and as unpredictable—thus the magic!

1. Fill the firing container with carbon, leaving 1 inch (2.5 cm) of space at the top.
2. Place the container on posts in the kiln so it's not sitting directly on the kiln floor. Leave off the container lid.
3. Fast ramp the kiln to 1650°F (899°C) and hold it there for 30 minutes. Let cool, and you are ready to do your first firing!

Making Test Strips

I cannot stress enough the importance of including a test strip in each firing. Just because pieces look sintered does not mean they are sintered. I usually make an extra component to use as the test piece. You should be able to bend a fired piece at least 90 degrees without it breaking or cracking. If it breaks, the piece was not fully sintered and must be re-fired. Here are some common firing issues and how to resolve them.

- If metal clay pieces come out of the firing with bubbles, the kiln was too hot. Lower the temperature by 50°F.
- If the surface of a piece is rough and grainy, lower the firing temperature in the kiln by 15°F.
- If a piece has small splits or cracks, slow down the heating time to 1000°F per hour.
- If a test piece breaks and the inside is powdery, the kiln temperature is too low. Raise it by 25°F. Keep raising the temperature by 25°F with each firing as needed until full sintering is achieved.
- If a test piece breaks but feels metallic rather than powdery, extend the hold time on the kiln by one hour.

Firing PMC Sterling

Two separate firings are necessary for PMC Sterling metal clay. First, you must fire off the binder. This can be done on an open shelf in the kiln or with a torch. Fast ramp the kiln to 1000°F (538°C) and hold the temperature for 30 minutes. If using a torch, place the metal clay on a firebrick or other fireproof surface and blast the piece with a torch to fire off the binder. You'll see the flame disintegrate the binder and flare up quite high. Once the flare subsides, the binder has been burned away and you can turn off the torch. Now you're ready for the second firing. Load the container and program the kiln to heat up at full speed until it reaches 1500°F (816°C). Hold this temperature for at least 30 minutes (two hours to be safe).

Firing PMC 3

To fire PMC 3, set the completed piece on a heatable tile or fiber brick and place it inside a kiln. Your best bet for firing this clay is to program your kiln to heat up at full speed until it reaches 1650°F (899°C) and hold the kiln at this temperature for two hours. (The minimum firing requirements are 1100°F [593°C] held for 30 minutes.)

Firing BRONZclay

BRONZclay needs to be kiln-fired in a stainless steel or ceramic container filled with activated carbon. Your best bet for firing this type of clay is to program your kiln to heat up at 250°F (121°C) per hour until it reaches 1550°F (843°) and hold this temperature for two hours.

Firing Fastfire BRONZclay

Most Fastfire BRONZclay pieces fire in two hours unless they're super thick. This clay must be buried in a stainless steel or ceramic container filled with activated carbon and kiln-fired. Fastfire BRONZclay fires more quickly than regular BRONZclay. I have not noticed any difference in the end result if fired properly. Program your kiln to ramp up at 1525°F (829°C) per hour until it reaches 1525°F (829°C) and hold this temperature for one hour. (Total kiln time is two hours.)

Firing COPPRclay

The rich color of copper and bronze is very fashion-forward and popular in today's jewelry trends. COPPRclay is fun to work with and much more affordable than her silver sister. You can even throw it on a potter's wheel to make larger pieces. You can enamel, patina, guild, and carve it. COPPRclay pieces need to be buried in a stainless steel or ceramic container filled with activated carbon and kiln-fired.

Cool Down

Always wait for the kiln to completely cool down before removing the metal clay pieces from the firing container. There will be a thin layer of ash on top of the carbon that needs to be sifted off, so put on your dust mask, head outside or into a well-ventilated area, and pour the carbon into another container. Alternately, use your fingers to sift through the carbon, picking out the fired metal clay pieces as you go. Pour the carbon back and forth between containers, and watch the ash fly away. I've found it helpful to keep a kiln-firing journal and write down how many pieces I put in the container before each firing. Once these pieces shrink, they may be hard to find as you sift through the carbon. Rinse off your pieces with water, and then shine them up in a tumbler or hand-polish them with a steel brush.

Torch Firing

I strongly suggest wearing appropriate safety glasses every time you torch fire.

1. Make certain the metal clay piece or pieces are completely dry, and then position them on a fiber brick (photo A).
2. Place the fiber brick on a piece of wood or concrete that is far from anything that can catch fire or singe.
3. Light the torch and move the flame back and forth about 1 inch (2.5 cm) away from the clay pieces (photo B). The pieces will flare up as the binder burns away. Don't panic! The flames will quickly go out, and the clay will soon begin to glow bright reddish-yellow (photo C). Keep this color as consistent as possible for five to ten minutes, and then turn off the torch. Let the fired pieces cool on their own.

A

Creating Patinas on Metal Clay

There are so many fun patinas to play with these days. Here are a few of my faves. Be sure to seal each patinated piece with some type of sealant to improve color permanence. Renaissance Wax Polish and Vintaj Sealer are the easiest and least toxic options for sealing metals and preventing oxidation. Clear Krylon is a good choice when you need a spray application.

Liver of Sulphur

Liver of sulphur (a.k.a. potassium sulfide) is a common solution used to blacken metal. It's a chemical coloring agent that smells horrid (unless you enjoy rotten eggs) but works beautifully on fired metal clay pieces. The process of applying patinas is not 100 percent guaranteed to have consistent results, so be prepared to experiment and have fun with the surprises! Liver of sulphur is sold in solid chunks that you mix with distilled water. It also comes in a liquid form and can be used right out of the bottle. Liver of sulphur needs to be stored in a dark, sealed bag to maintain its strength.

B

Applying a Liver of Sulphur Patina

1. Clean the metal clay piece with soapy water and a soft brush. Resist touching it with your fingers. I use tweezers for the process.
2. Mix the liver of sulphur solution (if needed) and heat it on a coffee cup warmer.
3. Dip the metal clay into the solution, and let the color develop for a few moments.
4. Remove the metal from the solution. Rinse or dip the metal into cold water to stop the color changing.
5. Repeat steps 3 and 4 until you're satisfied with the color of the patina.

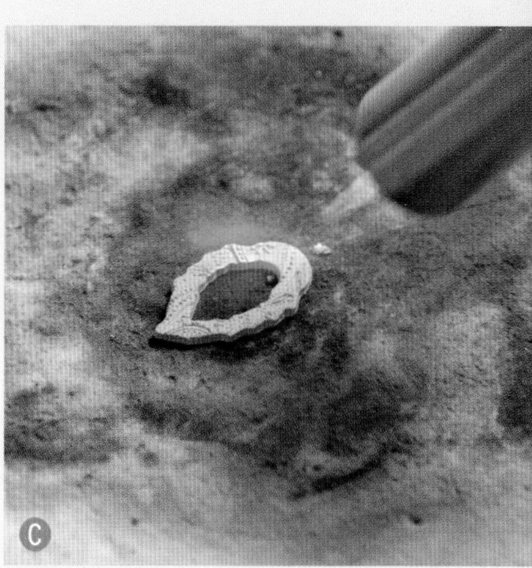

C

Miracle-Gro (Plant Food)

This is a fun patina that creates very pretty blue color, but it only works on copper.

1. Mix a 50/50 solution of Miracle-Gro and water.
2. Spray the solution on fired copper pieces, and wait at least 24 hours.
3. Rinse, dry, and seal the colored metal clay.

Baroque Art Gilders Paste

Rub or brush Baroque Art Gilders Paste on a piece of fired metal clay. Wait 12 hours until the paste completely cures, and then seal the finish. Layering paste colors can create some spectacular effects. If you polish the metallic pastes with a soft cloth once they are cured, the result is a gilded finish similar to gold leaf. If you leave the paste unpolished, the finish has a more matte look.

Vintaj Patinas

My latest favorite patinas come from the Vintaj collection. These are opaque inks specifically formulated for metal, and they come in gorgeous colors. Sold in sets of three, each combination was developed to emulate natural patinas over time. They can be layered, blended, and then sanded off for some fascinating effects. They also come with a glaze that can also be used as a sealer and an extender to dilute the bright patina colors if desired.

Jax Patinas

This commercial patina is sold in many super colors, and it can be painted on directly from the bottle. Let Jax patinas sit on fired metal clay for two or more hours, and then rinse, dry, and seal the piece.

Hard-Boiled Egg Patina

Put a warm, peeled, hard-boiled egg in a plastic bag with a fired piece of metal clay, seal the bag tightly, and let it sit for a few hours. When you like the color that has developed, remove and seal the metal.

Swarovski crystals

Embellishments

At long last, when you're finally putting together your metal clay and beaded jewelry, here are the lovely embellishments, components, and assorted doodads you'll need to make it wearable and beautiful, too!

Beads

You can never have too many shoes, chocolates, and BEADS! A bead is anything with a hole through it that you can string onto beading thread or wire. Whether made of stone, glass, bone, shell, crystal, or—my personal fave—fabric, beads are the mother ship of jewelry making. From filler to focal, beads can be used in so many ways. Here are details on the beads I used for the projects in this book.

Seed Beads

The tiniest and the most addictive in my opinion, seed bead is a generic term for any small bead. Seed beads come in a wide variety of colors, shapes, and sizes. The smaller the number, the larger the bead. Sizes 8° and 11° are great for peyote and herringbone stitches. I like to use donut-shaped seed beads for a consistent, snug fit when stitching.

Bugle beads are long, thin tubes of glass, and the edges can be very sharp, so watch your beading threads! Rocailles are taller than regular seed beads and are also fun to work with. Square seed beads add a slightly architectural element to beaded designs, so be sure to experiment with them as well.

There are many types of finishes and coatings on seed beads. Matte means the bead is textured and not shiny. Transparent and translucent means you can see light coming through the bead. This is the opposite of opaque, which means the bead is one solid color. Silver-lined seed beads have a silvery layer on the interior of the bead. Similarly, copper-lined beads have a copper-colored layer inside. Luster means the bead has a smooth, pearlescent effect. AB (Aurora Borealis) seed beads have a rainbow coloration on the surface that resembles an oil spill.

Fabric Beads

Near and dear to my heart are fabric beads. This variety can be made out of silk, like my Sassy Silkies, or made out of batik fabrics. They add an entirely different texture to your jewelry creations.

Crystal Beads

The Cadillac of all crystal beads is made by Swarovski in Austria. No other crystal bead achieves a similar brilliance and sparkle, which is why they're my favorites!

Chatons

Chatons are pointed-back crystals made by Swarovski. The back surface is covered with foil, and this produces the ultimate in color reflection. Chatons are perfect for gluing into fired metal clay creations with two-part epoxy. I receive the most successful results from Devcon 5- or 30-minute epoxy.

Flat Back Crystals

Sometimes referred to as rhinestones, flat back crystals are similar to chatons, only they have a foiled, flat back instead of a point. If you plan to glue chatons into a fired piece but the holes shrink too much, simply substitute flat back crystals and use two-part epoxy to adhere them.

Marbled Ceramic Fancy Stones

Swarovski manufactures these embellishments in a limited variety of shapes, sizes, and marbled colors. They add a sleek style to jewelry creations and are perfect for an earthier look—a rich component without the bling.

Semiprecious Gemstone Chips

Semiprecious chips are readily available in hundreds of different stones, colors, sizes, and shapes. The tiny chips are an inexpensive alternative to the larger stones, and I like to use them to achieve a similar effect.

Pearls

Spacer beads

Pearls

The beloved pearl has been popular for eons with good reason. They are quite simply marvelous! Both cultured and natural pearls have very small holes. You may need a bead reamer to make the holes larger. Swarovski glass pearls are my fave due to their consistent holes and sizes.

Spacer Beads

Spacer beads are a fundamental component often used in beaded jewelry. Place them between beads to add shine, dimension, and sharpness. Spacer beads are available in a range of metals, from base to precious, and many styles, sizes, and prices to fit every budget.

Bead Caps

Use bead caps with any basic bead to add an ornate design element. Some bead caps fit tightly to the bead. Others caps sit slightly apart from a bead to increase length and enhance decoration. Filigree and other openwork bead caps let colorful beads show through.

Pendants

Commercial pendants serve as focal elements for necklaces. The variety of pendants available is massive and growing every day. Metal, ceramic, wood, glass, stone, plastic—if you want it, there's a good chance someone makes it. Some pendants, such as empty frames and bezels, are intended to be customized. Most pendants require bails to be functional.

Pendant

Dangles & Charms

These commercial decorative elements are an easy way to increase the visual impact of your jewelry. They are manufactured in popular shapes such as flowers, hearts, leaves, and stars. Dangles and charms can be simple and smooth die-cut forms or complex cast shapes with intricate textures. These components have pre-existing holes making them easy to attach to jewelry with jump rings.

Beading Wire

Beading wire consists of many thin steel wires tightly wound together inside a nylon coating. It's used for stringing and is available in many different colors. The fewer the strands, the stiffer the drape. The thicker the dimension, the stronger the wire. Use matching crimps for finishing off wire ends.

Beading Thread

There are many varieties of beading thread, made from materials such as silk, nylon, and the ever-popular Tiger Tail. I recommend using a strong, braided beading thread for bead weaving. Sharp edges on crystals, pearls, and gemstones can cut thread easily. Stick with the strongest type you can find, such as Wildfire or Fireline.

Needles

Beading needles are longer and thinner than sewing needles. The larger the number, the thinner the needle. With practice, you'll discover the perfect needle for you, and stick with it (pardon the pun) for consistent results. Remember, you get what you pay for, so don't skimp on quality here. I think English beading needles rock!

Bead Stoppers

I absolutely love bead stoppers, and once you use them you'll be a fan as well! A bead stopper is a small spring with little handles. When you squeeze the spring, it opens and you can slip it onto your beading wire. The spring automatically closes over the thread. This allows you to string beads onto the other end of the thread without them flying onto the floor. Your vacuum thanks you!

Sticky Mats

If I were asked which beading supplies would be a must when deserted on a tropical island, sticky mats run neck-and-neck with bead stoppers. Any type of bead or crystal will stay put when placed on a sticky mat; hence it is great for traveling. Just remember that cat hair sticks just as well as bicones! To reactivate the stickiness of a mat, simply rinse it off with cold water and let dry.

Crimp Tubes & Crimp Beads

The long debate over the merits of crimp tubes versus crimp beads continues. Personally, I like both for different reasons. Because crimp tubes are longer, they have more interior surface area to grip the wire, making them stronger than crimp beads. (When making a particularly heavy necklace, you may want to double crimp the ends for added security.) Crimp beads are inexpensive and less noticeable. The recommended crimp bead or tube size for a beading wire is generally listed on its spool. Use crimp covers to hide crimp tubes or beads as desired.

Beading wire

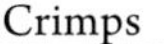

Crimps

Jewelry Components and Tools

Components, also known as findings, are the staples for making wearable, functional jewelry. They are the basic elements that hold, link, clasp, finish, and decorate parts of your designs.

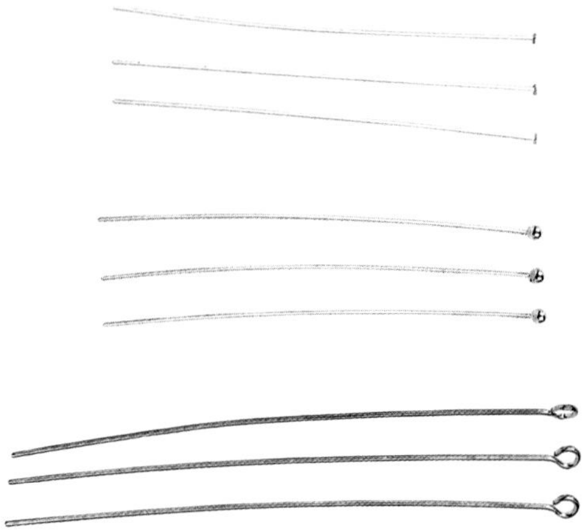

Metal Wire

Use metal wire for wire wrapping and making links. Metal wire is sold in a wide variety of gauges (thicknesses) and colors. Colored wire is usually copper that's been coated with a few layers of colored enamel. When wrapping colored wire, use pliers with a nylon jaw so the color doesn't scratch off.

Head pins

A head pin is a jewelry component that looks like a little wire pole with a flat end, a feature that serves as a stopper for beads. Head pins are available in many different metals, colors, and gauges. A head pin with a little decorative ball at the end is called a ball headpin.

Eye Pins

Eye pins are jewelry findings similar to head pins but they have a loop rather than a flat stopper at one end. You can add dangles or link other elements through this loop. Purchase eye pins ready-made or easily create your own by forming a loop at one end of a wire.

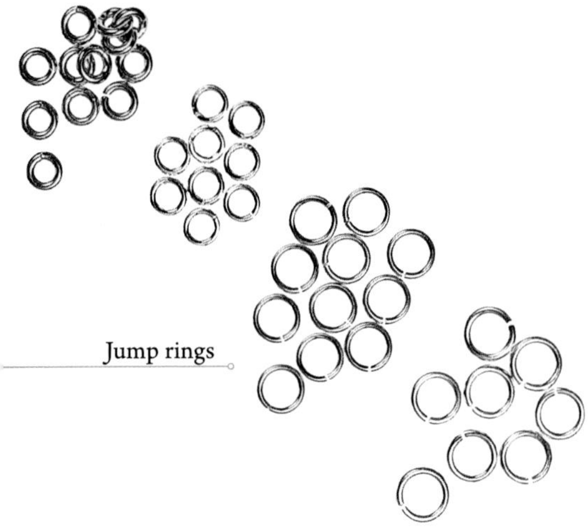

Jump Rings

Jump rings are an essential component for assembling jewelry parts. You can make your own jump rings fairly easily or purchase large packages of ready-made rings. (I buy jump rings to save time—I like to jump into the fun part of jewelry making!) Ready-made jump rings are available in many metals, finishes, and sizes. They also come in a few different shapes, such as round, oval, and triangular. I particularly like using twisted jump rings for added texture.

Chain

Chains made of different metals with different finishes have become really trendy these days. I encourage you to mix it up when using chains. Step off the silver "path," and add a strand or two of bronze or copper for added color.

Clasps & Toggles

Finish off a necklace or bracelet with a decorative (and functional!) clasp. There are beautiful commercial clasps in the marketplace. Lobster, magnetic, toggle, hook & eye, trigger, swivel, mult-strand, spring ring, and S hooks are just some of the most popular designs. Clasps add the last splash of elegance to your jewelry creations. Toggle clasps have two parts: a T-shaped bar and a ring. To close the clasp, the bar end is pulled through the open loop. This clasp design is very popular and easy to use.

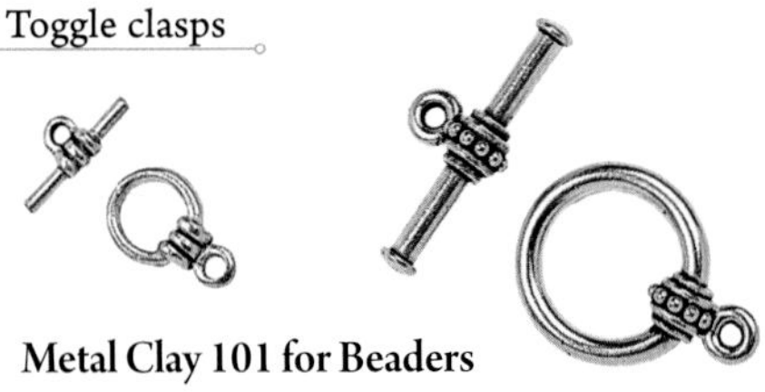

Bails

A bail is a necklace component used to attach a pendant. A bail is attached in the center of a necklace where the pendant traditionally hangs. Use a bail to easily turn your favorite beads and charms into pendants.

Head pins and eye pins

Jump rings

Lobster clasps

Toggle clasps

Ear Wires

Purchase ready-made ear wires or make your own custom designs with wire and pliers or a wig jig. To eliminate most chances of skin allergies, use sterling silver, gold, or gold-filled wires for any component that goes through the ear.

Pliers

Chain-nose pliers have pointed tips and smooth, flat jaws. Use these for pulling your beading needle through a tight stitch, opening jump rings, making wrapped loops, and more.

Round-nose pliers have round jaws that taper toward the tips. Use them when making wire loops. To make your loops a consistent size, mark a location on a jaw of the pliers with a permanent marker.

Flat-nose pliers are similar to chain-nose pliers but with wider jaws. Use flat-nose pliers to grip wire, make wrapped loops, and open jump rings. Some pliers come with nylon-coated jaws that deter you from making scratches on the surface of colored wires.

Crimping pliers are specifically used to finish the ends of a strung piece of jewelry. The pliers tighten crimping beads in a precise manner that secures the stringing. Regular jewelry pliers, such as needle or round nose, cannot be substituted for crimping pliers. They will not make a secure crimp.

Wire Cutters

I always use wire cutters for thread as well as wire because the edge turns out clean and nonfraying. Scissors can be used to cut nylon and silk beading thread, but the result is not as neat.

Ear wires

Chain-nose pliers

Flat-nose pliers

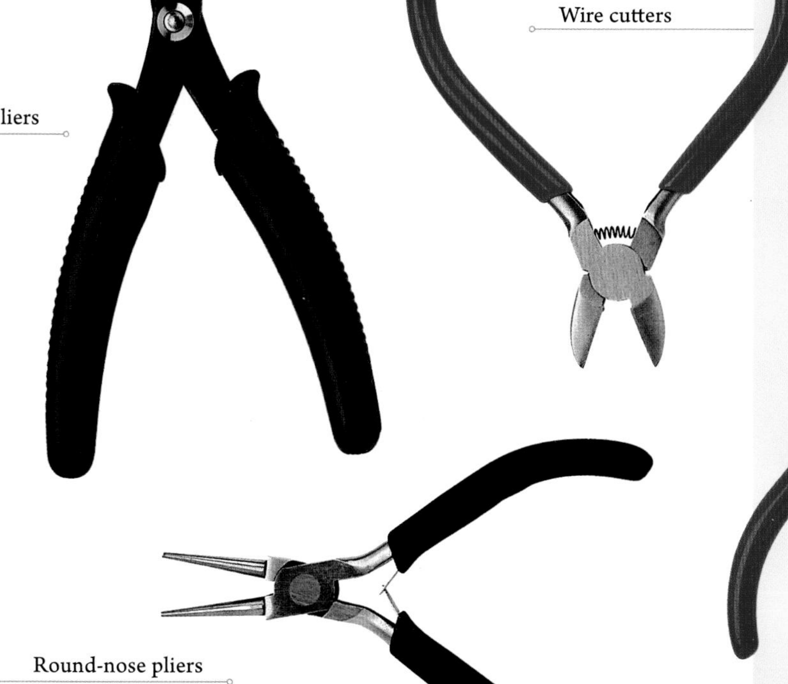

Wire cutters

Crimping pliers

Round-nose pliers

Bead Stringing and Stitches

Learning to string beads in a high quality, professional manner is very simple. Taking the little extra time and effort will serve you and your handmade jewelry well.

1. Cut a length of beading wire that is at least 5 inches (12. cm) longer than the length of your beading project.

TIP

```
When cutting beading wire, it's always better
to err on the side of caution with a length
clearly longer than what's required.
```

2. Thread the following elements onto one end of the beading wire in this order: project beads, crimp bead or tube, connection finding (the clasp loop for example).
3. Pass the beading wire back through the crimp and a few beads, pulling the beading wire tight but leaving a small loop so the connection finding is free to move.
4. Position the crimp in the back notch of the crimping tool and press the crimp down between the wires. (See page 37 for more on Crimping.) The crimp side will fold up a bit and look like a mini taco.
5. Rotate the crimp 90 degrees, position it in the front notch of the crimping tool, and press to fold the taco closed. Trim any excess wire.
6. String the jewelry components following the sequence in the project directions.
7. Thread the last element onto the other end of the beading wire, then add a crimp bead or tube and the connection finding (the clasp for example).
8. Pass the beading wire back through the crimp and a few beads, pulling the beading wire tight but leaving a small loop so the connection finding is free to move.
9. Position the crimp in the back notch of the crimping tool and press the crimp down between the wires.
10. Rotate the crimp 90 degrees, position it in the front notch of the crimping tool, and press to fold the crimp closed. Trim any excess wire.

Ladder Stitch Directions

The ladder stitch is a basic foundation stitch in bead weaving. It creates a single row of woven beads. Use it as base from which to start the tubular herringbone used in the Tubular Herringbone Necklace with Flower on page 89 and Russian Rhapsody Herringbone Lariat on page 60. Here are instructions for stitching the traditional ladder, which is a single-needle, single-thread stitch technique.

1. Cut approximately 6 feet (1.83 m) of beading thread, and thread the needle.
2. String the first two beads on the needle.
3. Pass the thread back through the first strung bead.
4. Pass the thread back through the second bead strung (figure 1). When you pull on the thread, this will form a circle with the thread and position the beads with their holes facing out.
5. Pick up the third bead with the needle, and then pass the thread through the second bead strung.
6. Pass the thread back through the last bead strung (figure 2).
7. Repeat this process—stringing a new bead, passing the thread back through the previous bead and then through the new bead—until you've woven the length desired.

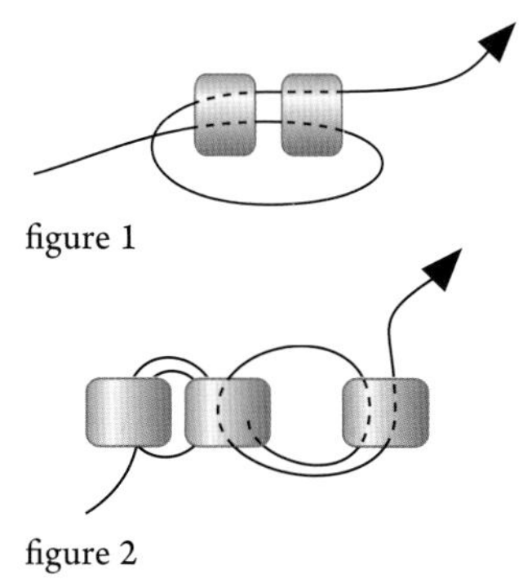

figure 1

figure 2

Ladder stitch

Tubular Herringbone Stitch Directions

Tubular herringbone is a versatile stitch that's easy to work up. Its tube shape drapes well and is a natural choice for jewelry, especially necklaces and bracelets.

1. Use the ladder stitch to make an even-number ladder of beads. The ladder should be four or more beads.
2. To sew the ladder into a ring, stitch up through the first ladder bead, back down through the last bead, and pull the thread tight. To completely secure the ring, stitch through the first bead again, then through the second bead.
3. Pick up two beads on the needle. Stitch down through the next bead in the ring. Stitch up through the following bead, and pull the thread tight (figure 3).
4. Repeat this herringbone stitch around the ring, adding two beads at a time. At the end of the ring, step-up through the ladder and first bead added in the round. Pull the thread tight (figure 4).

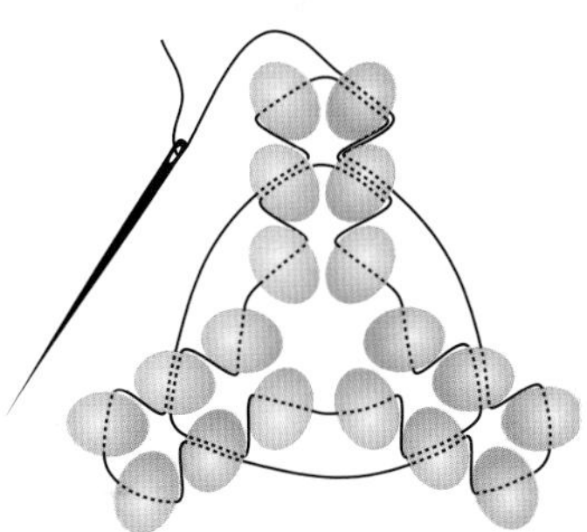

figure 3

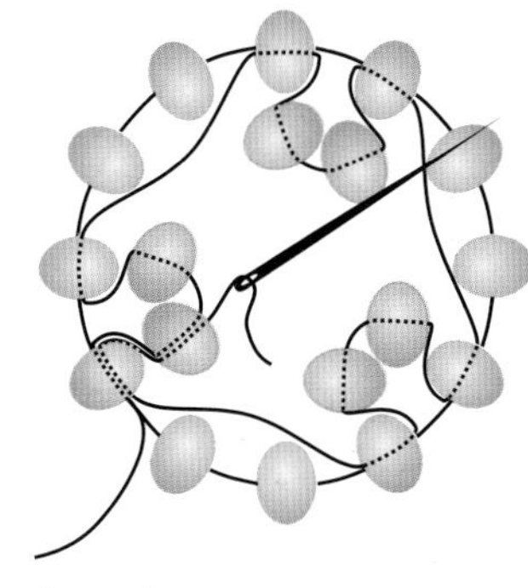

figure 4

Tubular herringbone

TIP

Until the tube takes a shape, you can steady your work by placing a pencil or a dowel inside the rings.

5. Continue adding rings of herringbone stitch, stepping up through two beads at the end of each ring.

When the herringbone tube is the desired length, finish the final ring by stepping-up into the second-to-last bead. Stitch down through the third bead, and up through the fourth, pulling tight with each pass. Continue around the tube until each bead is secure and tie off with a double knot.

Odd-Count Peyote Stitch Directions

This beading stitch creates woven strips perfect for bracelets and necklaces. Use these instructions when making the Peyote Cuff with Metal Leaves (page 69), the Peyote Stitch Bracelet with Magnetic Clasp (page 57), and the Peyote Stitch Buckle Bracelet (page 112).

1. Cut a comfortable length of working thread. (The longer the thread, the more you can stitch before needing to add a new thread.)
2. String beads onto the thread to make the first row (figure 1). The number of beads varies per project, but it should be an odd number.
3. String one bead, pass the needle through the next-to-last strung bead, and then pull the thread to tighten the beads.
4. String one bead, skip the next bead in the row, and then pass the needle through the bead after the one skipped. Pull the thread to tighten the beads. Continue adding beads until you've reached the end of the row (figure 2).
5. Turn around the beading so you can work in the same direction as the previous row.
6. String one bead, and pass the needle through the first raised bead. Continue picking up one bead and passing the needle through a raised bead (figure 3). Stitch across the row.
7. Repeat this peyote stitch pattern to create the length required by the project instructions (figure 4).

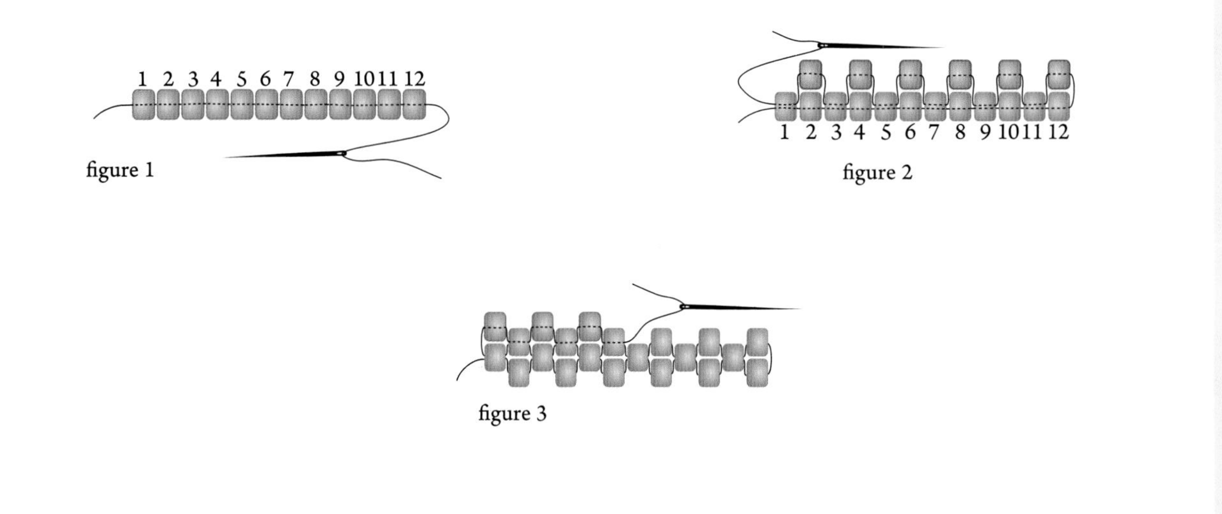

Peyote stitch

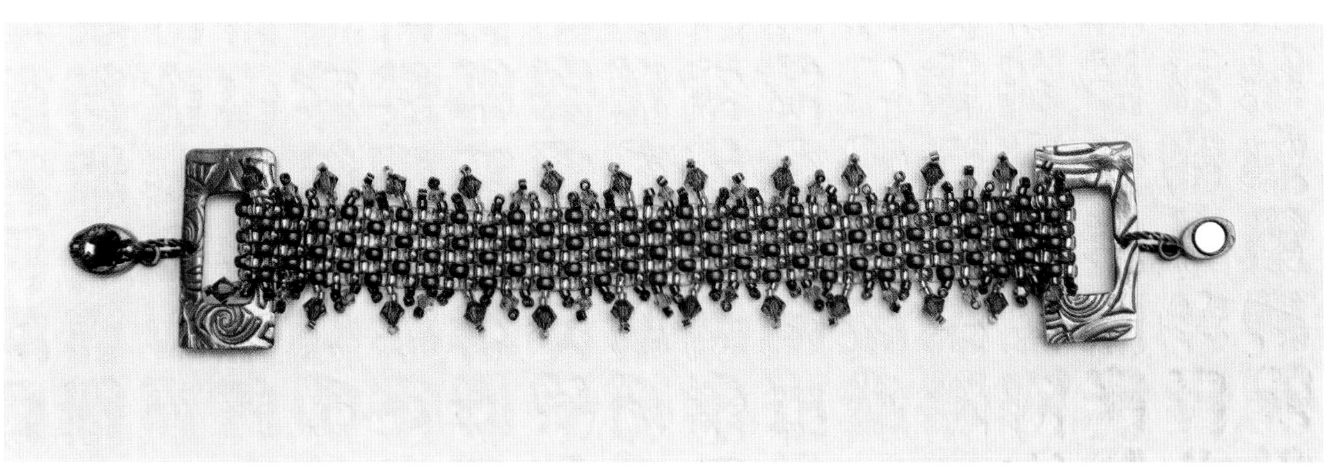

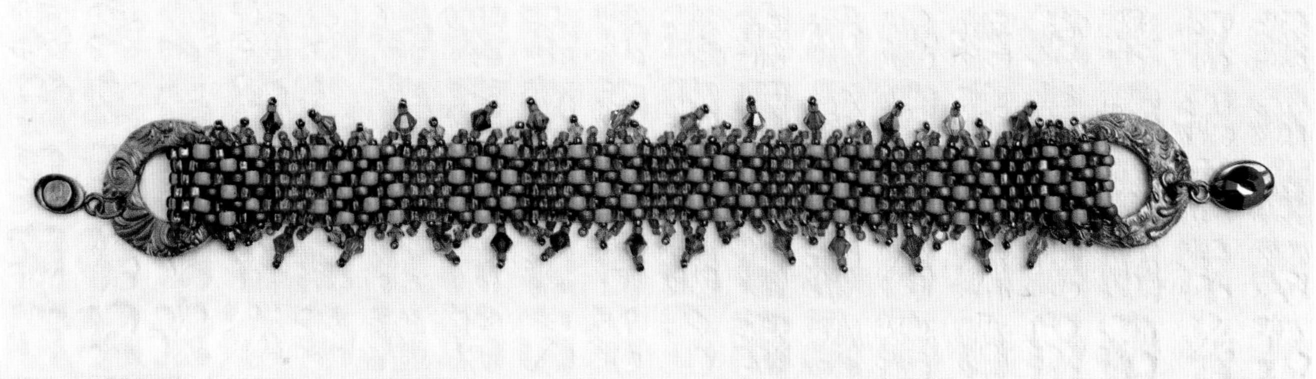

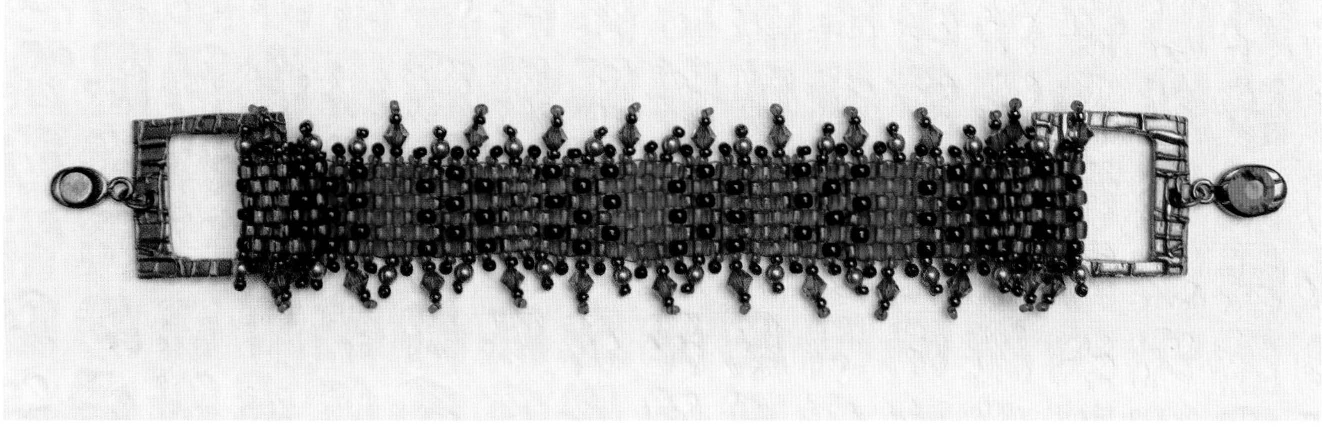

Basic Wire Techniques

Opening and Closing Jump Rings

Grip the jump ring on both sides of the split using chain- or flat-nose pliers. Rotate one hand toward you and the other away from you so you are twisting the ring open, not pulling the ends apart (figure 1). Close the jump ring using the same motion, making sure the split is closed tightly.

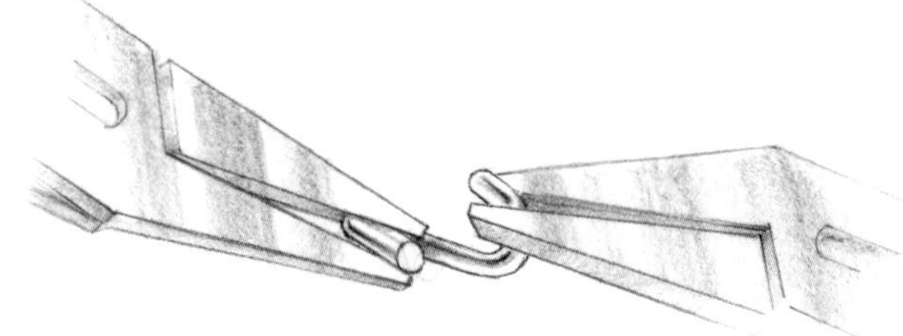

figure 1

Simple Loops and Bead Loop Links

Practice makes perfect when it comes to making loops, so if you're new to jewelry making, just keep on looping and you'll have professional-looking loops in no time!

1. Use flat- or chain-nose pliers to bend the wire to a 90° angle (figure 2).
2. Cut the wire, leaving about ½ inch (1.3 cm)—the length depends on how large a loop you desire.
3. Grasp the end of the wire with round-nose pliers and rotate the pliers to form a loop (figure 3). Tweak the loop if needed to center it (figure 4).
4. To make a bead loop link (figure 5), simply repeat these steps to enclose a bead (or beads) between two loops.

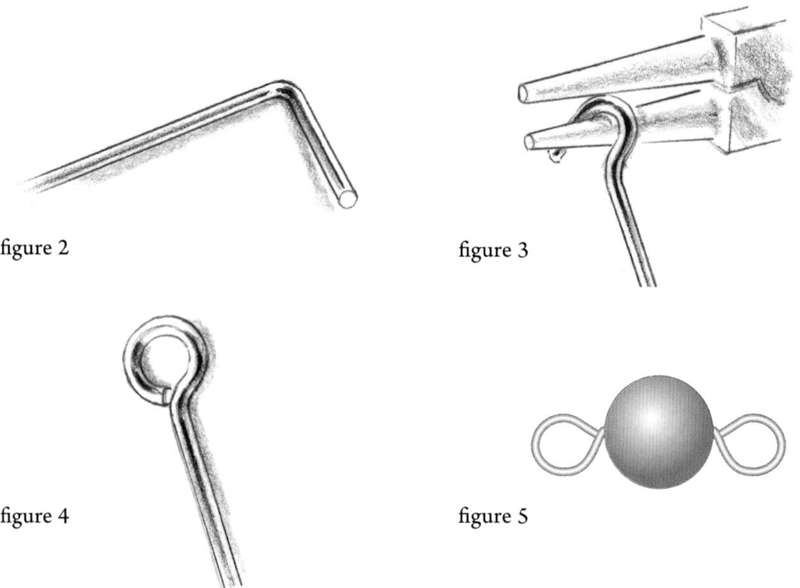

figure 2

figure 3

figure 4

figure 5

Wrapped Loops and Wrapped Bead Loop Links

As shown in figure 6, the wrapped loop is a variation of the simple loop just described. Use an extra length of wire for the 90° bend. Once you've made the loop, reposition the pliers so that the lower jaw is inside it. Using your other hand and keeping the wire at a right angle as you work, wrap the wire tail around the neck of the wire two or three times. Cut the wire, and then tuck the end close to the remaining length.

To make a wrapped bead loop link (figure 7), simply repeat these steps to enclose a bead (or beads) between two wrapped loops.

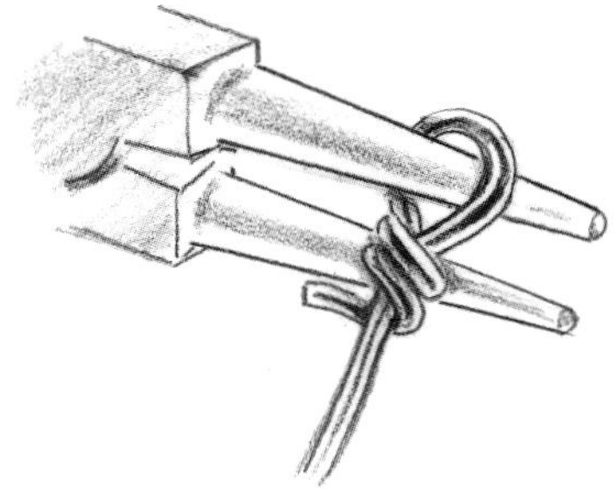

figure 6

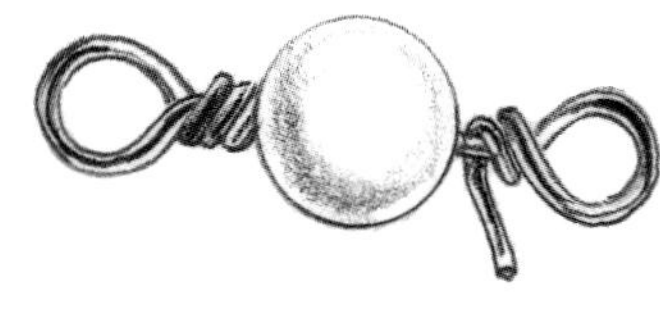

figure 7

Crimping

Crimp tubes are great for attaching findings to beading wire. As shown in figure 8, the jaw of a pair of crimping pliers has two notches: one is U shaped and the other is oval.

1. String a crimp tube and then the finding onto the wire. Thread the wire back through the crimp tube in the opposite direction.
2. To secure the crimp tube, fit the crimp into the U-shaped notch (the notch furthest from the pliers' tip) and squeeze.
3. Rotate the crimp tube 90° and place it inside the oval notch. Squeeze the pliers so the crimp tube folds in on itself into a nicely shaped tube.

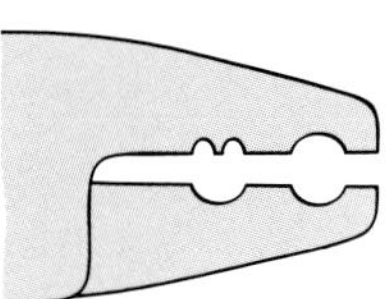

figure 8

birdhouse necklace

As the kick-off project for this book, my friend Chris and I spent hours making these adorable birdhouses and simply could not stop. Highly addictive, they remind us of springtime and the sweet songs of birds.

WHAT YOU NEED

- Metal clay toolbox, page 14
- Copper or bronze clay
- Cookie cutters: assorted shapes, such as flowers, leaves, butterflies, and squares
- Two-part epoxy
- Flat back crystals or chatons
- Beading wire, 1⁄55 inch (0.46 mm), copper
- Chain- or flat-nose pliers, 2 pairs
- Head pin, copper
- 2 jump rings
- Crystal bicones, 3 mm
  - 6 purple velvet
  - 2 copper
  - 68 Colorado light topaz
  - 8 cyclamen opal
- Crystal bicones, 4 mm
  - 1 lavender
  - 3 Colorado light topaz
  - 32 cyclamen opal
- Crystal butterfly, 5 mm, lavender
- Butterfly charm, copper
- Crystal round, 6 mm, violet
- Colorado light topaz briolette drop, 5 mm
- 37 crystal pearls, 4 mm, antique brass
- 2 crimps, copper
- Crimping tool
- 2 eye pins, copper

HOW TO MAKE IT

Building the Birdhouse

Place the metal clay on top of a texture plate, and roll it out 4 cards thick. Carefully remove the clay from the texture plate. As shown in photo A, cut out two squares, a picket fence post, and two roof liners. Use cookie cutters to cut out small embellishments. Cut a heart shape out of the middle of one of the metal clay squares for the doorway.

As shown in photo B, trim the bottom corner of both large squares on a diagonal, making sure they line up on top of each other when stacked. Let all of the clay pieces dry.

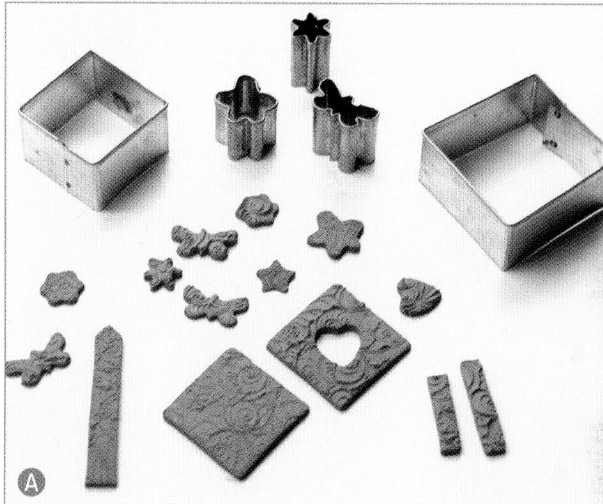

A

B

birdhouse necklace

Drill a hole in the top and the bottom of the picket fence post. Determine where you want to glue flat back crystals or chatons on the clay embellishments after they are fired, and drill slight indentations at these locations.

Stack the square with the heart cutout on top of the solid square, and attach the layers with lots of slip. Trim the roof liners to fit the roof, and attach them to the stacked squares with slip. Fill in the cracks between all layers of the entire birdhouse with slip (photo C). Attach the embellishments to the birdhouse with lots of slip (photo D). Attach the fencepost to the back of the birdhouse with lots of slip. Let all pieces dry completely.

NOTE

Did I mention using lots of slip once or twice? Thick slip acts like glue in metal clay firing. You want to use enough slip so your attachments solidify in the firing, but not so much that the slip oozes out around the sides. No worries if your attachments pop off when fired; simply reattach them using two-part epoxy after everything is tumbled.

Place the dry clay birdhouse in activated coconut carbon. Following the manufacturer's instructions, fire the birdhouse in the kiln. Tumble the fired birdhouse until you are satisfied with its polish. Using two-part epoxy, glue the flat back crystals or chatons into the indentations.

C

D

Forming the Dangles

Thread the beads and charms onto a head pin or eye pin in the order listed, and then form a simple loop at the top of each with pliers. Attach each dangle to the bottom hole in the picket fence with a jump ring.

Dangle 1 (eye pin)

Purple velvet crystal bicone, 3 mm
Colorado light topaz crystal bicone, 4 mm
Purple velvet crystal bicone, 3 mm
Lavender crystal butterfly, 5 mm
Purple velvet crystal bicone, 3 mm
Lavender crystal bicone, 4 mm
Copper crystal bicone, 3 mm
Copper butterfly charm (attach to the bottom eye-pin loop)

Dangle 2 (eye pin)

Purple velvet crystal bicone, 3 mm
Copper crystal bicone, 3 mm
Violet crystal round, 6 mm
Copper crystal bicone, 3 mm
Colorado light topaz briolette drop, 5 mm (attach to the bottom eye-pin loop)

Dangle 3 (head pin)

Purple velvet crystal bicone, 3 mm
Antique brass pearl, 4 mm
Purple velvet crystal bicone, 3 mm

birdhouse necklace

Stringing the Necklace

String the beads and pearls onto the copper beading wire in the following order:

Colorado light topaz crystal bicone, 4 mm
Colorado light topaz crystal bicone, 3 mm
Cyclamen opal crystal bicone, 3 mm
Antique brass pearl, 4 mm
Cyclamen opal crystal bicone, 3 mm
Colorado light topaz crystal bicone, 3 mm
Cyclamen opal crystal bicone, 3 mm
Antique brass pearl, 4 mm
Cyclamen opal crystal bicone, 3 mm
Colorado light topaz crystal bicone, 3 mm

Now string the following series 32 times:

Antique brass pearl, 4 mm
Colorado light topaz crystal bicone, 3 mm
Cyclamen opal crystal bicone, 4 mm
Colorado light topaz crystal bicone, 3 mm

Now string the following to finish:

Cyclamen opal crystal bicone, 3 mm
Antique brass pearl, 4 mm
Cyclamen opal crystal bicone, 3 mm
Colorado light topaz crystal bicone, 3 mm
Cyclamen opal crystal bicone, 3 mm
Antique brass pearl, 4 mm
Cyclamen opal crystal bicone, 3 mm
Colorado light topaz crystal bicone, 3 mm
Colorado light topaz crystal bicone, 4 mm

Crimp each end of the beaded necklace, leaving a small loop of wire at the top of the crimp. Use jump rings to attach the clasp ends to each necklace end. Use the large copper twisted jump ring to attach the birdhouse pendant to the center of the beaded necklace through the hole at the top of the picket fence.

picket fencepost earrings

Such a fun set when created in conjunction with the Birdhouse Necklace! The picket fenceposts give these earrings a rustic yet classy look sure to please all your nature-loving friends.

WHAT YOU NEED

Metal clay toolbox, page 14
Copper clay
4 antique copper jump rings, 6 mm
2 blue crystal chatons
2 copper ear wires
2 antique copper head pins, 1½ inches (3.8 cm)
4 copper crystal bicones, 3 mm
2 blue crystal bicones, 4 mm
Cookie cutters: leaf and flower shapes
2 pairs chain- or flat-nose pliers
Round-nose pliers
Tweezers
Wire cutters
Two-part epoxy

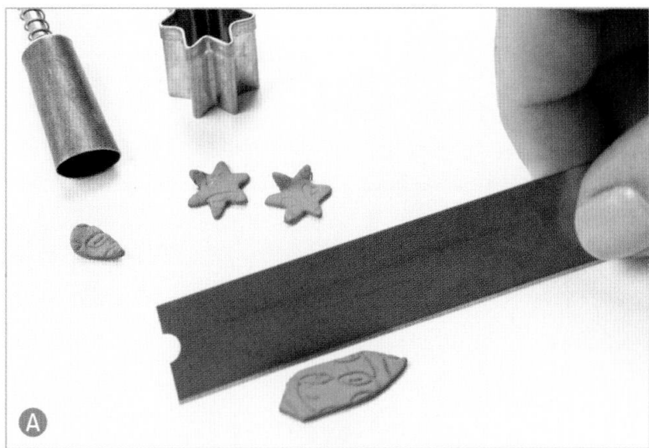
A

B

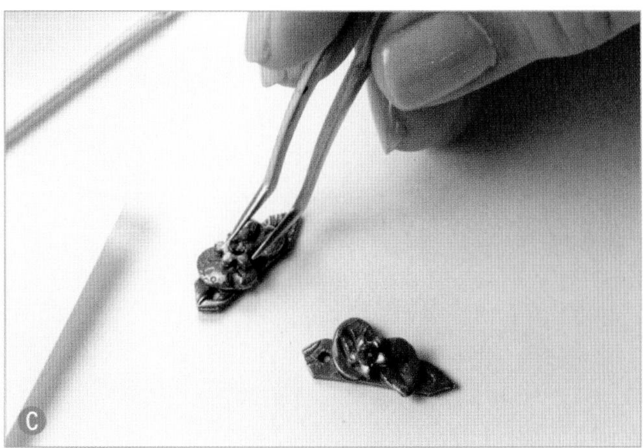
C

D

HOW TO MAKE IT

Place the clay on top of a texture plate, and roll it out four-cards thick. Carefully remove the clay from the texture plate. Cut out four clay leaves and four clay flowers with the cookie cutters. As shown in photo A, cut out two clay shapes resembling fence posts. Let all clay shapes dry.

Using a craft knife, make holes at the top and bottom of each fencepost. Attach the leaves and flowers to each fencepost using slip (photo B).

Carve a small indentation in the middle of each flower. (You'll adhere the chatons into these indentions later.)

Place the dry clay pieces in activated coconut carbon. Fire them in the kiln following the manufacturer's directions.

Tumble the fired pieces until you're satisfied with their polish. Use two-part epoxy to adhere a chaton to each flower (photo C).

String a copper bicone, a blue bicone, and another copper bicone onto a head pin, and then finish it off with a wrapped loop. Repeat this process to make a second beaded dangle. As shown in photo D, attach each dangle to the bottom of a fencepost with a jump ring. Attach an ear wire to the top of each fencepost with a jump ring.

heart necklace

All handcrafted jewelry comes from the heart, in my opinion, so feel free to take this phrase literally when making this necklace.

WHAT YOU NEED

- Metal clay toolbox, page 14
- Silver clay
- Card stock or heavy paper
- Cookie cutters: small flowers and small leaf
- Stiff paintbrush
- Mineral spirits
- Gilders paste in African Bronze, Patina, Pinotage, Iris Blue, Copper
- Two-part epoxy
- 5 flat back crystals, assorted sizes and colors
- 2 crimps
- Beading wire, 1/52 inch (0.48 mm), satin silver
- 24 crystal pearls, 6 mm, light green
- 22 crystal pearls, 5 mm, light green
- 22 crystal pearls, 8 mm, light gray
- 2 crystal pearls, 4 mm, dark gray
- 20 bead bumpers, silver
- 32 crystal bicones, 3 mm, black
- 6 crystal bicones, 6 mm, top drilled, peridot
- 6 crystal bicones, 6 mm, top drilled, rose
- 6 crystal bicones, 6 mm, top drilled, jonquil
- 4 crystal bicones, 6 mm, top drilled, blue
- 4 crystal bicones, 6 mm, top drilled, hyacinth
- 4 crystal bicones, 6 mm, top drilled, crystal
- Crystal circle, 20 mm
- Toggle bar, black
- 2 jump rings, 6 mm, black
- Crimping pliers
- Twist jump ring, 10 mm, silver
- 2 twist jump rings, 12 mm, silver

HOW TO MAKE IT

Make a drawing of a heart on card stock or heavy paper. Cut out the drawing to use as a template. Place the metal clay on a texture plate, and roll it 4 cards thick. Carefully remove the clay from the texture plate. Use the template to cut out the heart shape (photo A). Use the cookie cutters to cut out some metal clay flowers and a leaf.

As shown in photo B, use slip to attach the flowers and leaf to the heart. Let all metal clay elements dry completely.

Place the metal clay heart on the kiln shelf, and fire according to the manufacturer's instructions. Tumble the fired heart until you're satisfied with the polish.

heart necklace

Dip the paintbrush into the mineral spirits, and make a puddle in the gilders paste color of your choice. Load the paintbrush with the paste, and paint it onto different sections of the heart, flowers, and leaf (photo C). Change colors as often as desired. Let the paste dry for at least 24 hours. If desired, slightly buff the dry paste off the metal.

Mix the two-part epoxy, and use it to glue the flat back crystals onto the heart as shown in photo D. Let the epoxy cure completely.

C

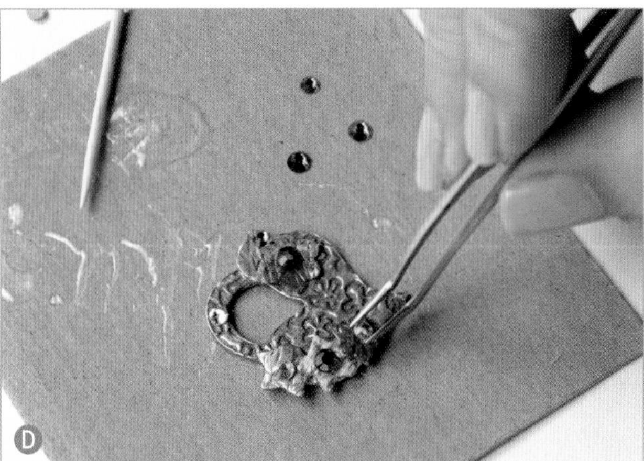

D

To create the necklace, string the beads onto the wire in the order that follows, and then crimp both ends, leaving a small loop.

Bead this sequence six times:

6 mm light green pearl
light gray pearl
6 mm light green pearl
black bicone

Continue stringing the necklace in this order:

5 mm light green pearl
light gray pearl
5 mm light green pearl
black bicone
bead bumper
peridot bicone
rose bicone
jonquil bicone
bead bumper
black bicone
5 mm light green pearl
light gray pearl
5 mm light green pearl
black bicone
bead bumper
blue bicone
crystal bicone
hyacinth bicone
bead bumper
black bicone
5 mm light green pearl
light gray pearl
5 mm light green pearl
black bicone
bead bumper
jonquil bicone
rose bicone
peridot bicone
bead bumper
black bicone
5 mm light green pearl

light gray pearl
5 mm light green pearl
black bicone
bead bumper
blue bicone
crystal bicone
hyacinth bicone
bead bumper
black bicone
5 mm light green pearl
light gray pearl
5 mm light green pearl
black bicone
bead bumper
jonquil bicone
rose bicone
peridot bicone
bead bumper
black bicone
5 mm light green pearl
2 dark gray pearls
5 mm light green pearl
black bicone
bead bumper
peridot bicone
rose bicone
jonquil bicone
bead bumper
black bicone
5 mm light green pearl
light gray pearl
5 mm light green pearl
black bicone
bead bumper
hyacinth bicone
crystal bicone
blue bicone
bead bumper
black bicone
5 mm light green pearl
light gray pearl
5 mm light green pearl
black bicone
bead bumper
peridot bicone
rose bicone
jonquil bicone
bead bumper
black bicone
5 mm light green pearl
light gray pearl
5 mm light green pearl
black bicone
bead bumper
hyacinth bicone
crystal bicone
blue bicone
bead bumper
black bicone
5 mm light green pearl
light gray pearl
5 mm light green pearl
black bicone
bead bumper
peridot bicone
rose bicone
jonquil bicone
bead bumper
black bicone
5 mm light green pearl
light gray pearl
5 mm light green pearl

Bead this sequence six times:

black bicone
5 mm light green pearl
light gray pearl
5 mm light green pearl

Attach the heart pendant to the center of the necklace using a large twist silver jump ring. Attach the crystal circle to one end of the necklace using a large twist silver jump ring. (I also added a sweet little heart charm to this ring.) On the opposite end of the necklace, attach a black jump ring, a twisted silver jump ring, and the toggle bar.

keycard lariat

I loved customizing my keycard lariat when I worked in a cubicle farm – and this beauty goes with everything you wear. You can leave off the lobster clasp and use the lariat as an eyeglass holder – simply slip one sidepiece through the center triangle to keep your glasses handy and stylish! Layering bisque beads is a great way to stretch your silver clay. There's no need to make solid silver beads; just coat any shape of bisque beads to make hollow silver ones.

WHAT YOU NEED

- Metal clay toolbox, page 14
- Silver clay
- Coffee stir straws
- Black permanent marker
- Polishing pads
- Chasing hammer
- 18 crystal bicones, 4 mm, AB
- 12 rondelles, 6 mm, jet
- 6 silver eye pins, 2 inches (5.1 cm)
- 3 black onyx leaf beads, 20 mm
- Extra large lobster clasp
- 11 marbled black rings, 14 mm
- 2 marbled black rings, 20 mm
- 4 bisque bead balls
- 2 bisque bead pillows
- Chain-nose pliers, two pairs
- Round-nose pliers
- Wire cutter
- 35 twisted jump rings, 12 mm

HOW TO MAKE IT

Place the metal clay on a texture plate, and roll out the clay 4 cards thick. Carefully remove the clay from the texture plate. Cut out six triangle-shaped frames. Select one frame to be the center of your lariat. Make two holes in this frame, each centered on a different point of the triangle. Let dry.

Fold the end of a stir straw in half, and tuck it into a bisque bead. Make sure it's a tight fit so you have a handle to hold when you coat the bead with clay. Repeat this with all bisque beads.

Water down the metal clay until it has a cream-like consistency. (You can use slip for this as well.) As shown in photo A, use a paintbrush to evenly apply six to eight coats of thinned silver clay around all bisque beads. Let each coat dry completely before applying the next one. When finished, carefully remove the stir straws from the beads. Use the same process to apply six to eight coats of thin clay to the inside rim of all bead holes. Let dry.

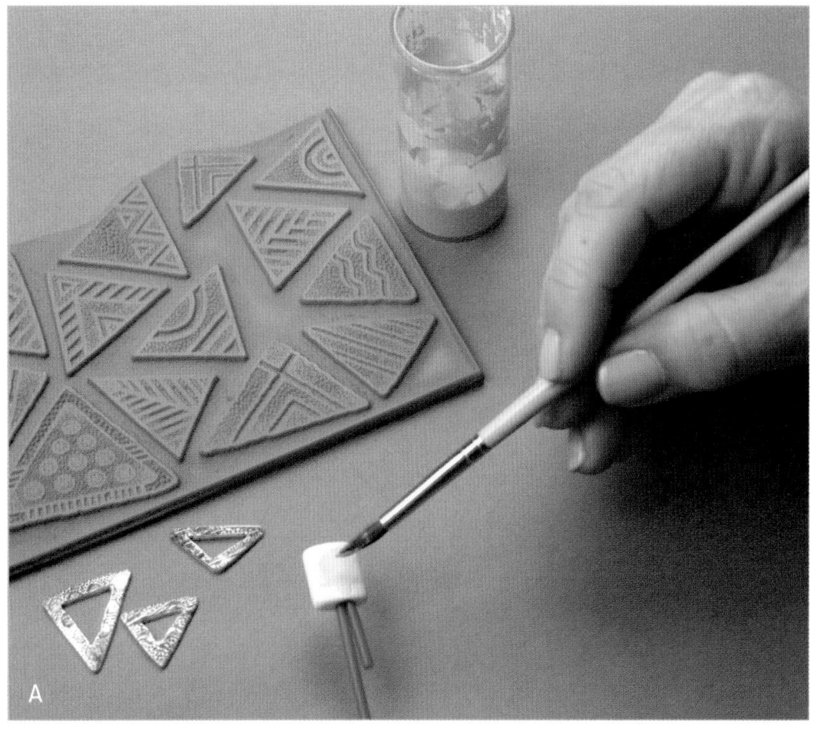
A

keycard lariat

Place the triangle frames and bisque beads on the kiln shelf and fire them, following the manufacturer's instructions. Tumble the fired components until you are satisfied with their polish. Color the triangle frames with a permanent black marker, and then buff off the excess color with polishing pads.

One at a time, place each bisque bead (with stir straw reinserted) on a hockey puck and use a chasing hammer to create texture on the bead (photo B). The surface of a hockey puck is firm enough for hammering the beads, but it also has a bit of give so the beads don't crack or distort when hammered.

To make the bisque bead links, string a crystal, a rondelle, a bisque bead, a second rondelle, and a second crystal onto an eye pin (photo C). Secure the link by bending a small loop after the last bead. Repeat this step to make links for all bisque beads.

To make the black onyx leaf links, string a crystal bicone, an onyx leaf, and a second crystal bicone onto an eye pin. Secure the link by bending a small loop after the last bead. Repeat this step to make links for all black onyx leaves.

Use twisted jump rings to connect the components in this order:

lobster clasp
center triangle frame
small marble ring
triangle frame
black leaf link
bisque ball link
large marble ring
small marble ring
triangle frame
bisque pillow link

B

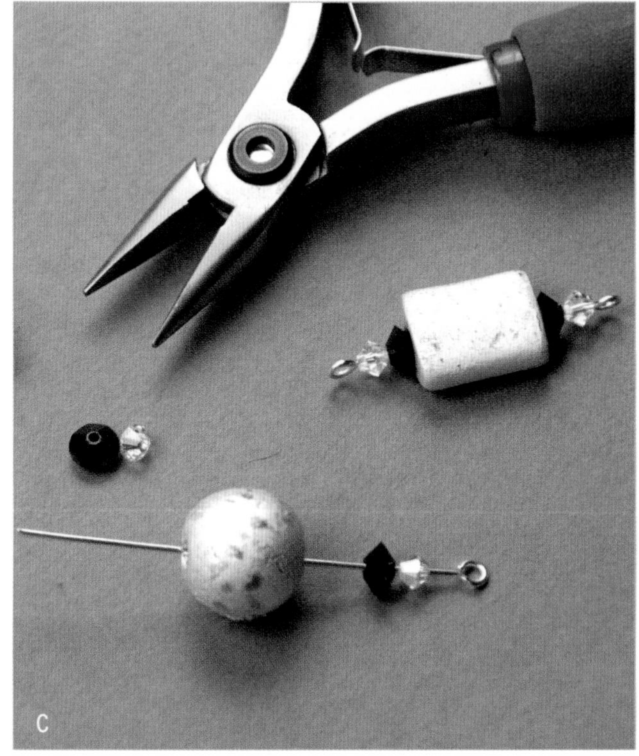
C

black leaf link
small marble ring
bisque ball link
5 small marble rings (use 2 twisted jump rings between each)
bisque ball link
large marble ring
triangle frame
bisque ball link
small marble ring
black leaf link
triangle frame
bisque pillow link
small marble ring
triangle frame
small marble ring
center triangle frame

puzzle bracelet

As a kid I was horrible at puzzles, but I never tire of this kind! It's a really fun piece to make with endless variations on the gemstone chips you use — certainly a showstopper!

WHAT YOU NEED

- Metal clay toolbox, page 14
- Copper clay
- Turquoise chips
- Two-part epoxy
- 8 large jump rings, seafoam
- 12 seed beads, size 11°, turquoise
- 12 seed beads, size 11°, copper
- 12 seed beads, size 11°, seafoam
- 20 small jump rings, seafoam
- 18 small jump rings, copper
- 12 large jump rings, copper
- 8 large jump rings, blue
- Toggle clasp
- Chain- or flat-nose pliers, 2 pairs

HOW TO MAKE IT

Place the metal clay on top of a texture plate, and roll out the clay 6 cards thick. Carefully remove the clay from the texture plate. Cut out a strip of clay that is 2 inches (5.1 cm) wide by 5 inches (12.7 cm) long. As shown in photo A, use a needle tool to randomly carve five puzzle pieces out of the single strip of clay, and let them completely dry.

Use a craft knife to make two holes near the narrow ends of each puzzle piece. Roll out a skinny clay snake. Use it to make five small ovals, one for each puzzle piece. Let the ovals dry. Attach one oval to each puzzle piece using lots of slip (photo B), and let dry.

Place the clay puzzle pieces in activated coconut carbon. Fire the clay in the kiln, following the manufacturer's instructions.

A

B

puzzle bracelet

Tumble the fired puzzle pieces until you're satisfied with their polish.

Make a pile of turquoise chips inside each oval on the fired puzzle pieces. Following the manufacturer's instructions, mix the two-part epoxy and then, as shown in photo C, use a toothpick to drop the adhesive on top of each pile of turquoise chips. Be extra careful not to overfill the ovals. Let the epoxy fully cure.

C

Use the large seafoam jump rings to attach the puzzle pieces in sequence, adding a seafoam, a copper, and a turquoise seed bead to each jump ring before closing (photo D).

Make a three-link chain, using a small copper jump ring and small seafoam jump ring for each link. Repeat this process to make a total of four short, double-link chains. Attach a chain to each of the large jump rings on both ends of the bracelet.

D

At one end of the bracelet, feed the last links of both three-link chains onto two large jump rings (one copper and one blue) and close the rings. Continue adding and then closing double rings to the end of the bracelet in this order:

2 small jump rings (one copper and one seafoam)
2 large jump rings (one copper and one blue)
2 small jump rings (one copper and one seafoam)
2 large jump rings (one copper and one blue)
2 small jump rings (one copper and one seafoam)
2 large jump rings (one copper and one blue)

Repeat this step on the opposite end of the bracelet. Use one small seafoam jump ring to attach the toggle to one end of the bracelet. Attach the bar to the opposite end of the bracelet with a small seafoam jump ring.

peyote stitch bracelet with magnetic clasp

These jazzy little ditties are as much fun to make as they are to wear! Embellish the edges of the bracelet with a glitzy fringe, and add some flare to the magnet clasp with an amethyst crystal. You'll love the elegant and flirty result.

peyote stitch bracelet with magnetic clasp

WHAT YOU NEED

- Metal clay toolbox, page 14
- Copper clay
- Cookie cutters: large and small rectangles
- Beading thread, 6 or 10 pound, dark color
- Beading needle, size 12°
- Seed beads, size 8°, 1 gram of each color: sage, violet, champagne
- Seed beads, size 15°, copper, gold
- At least 22 crystal bicones, 4 mm, amethyst
- At least 26 crystal bicones, 3 mm, Colorado light topaz
- Two-part epoxy
- Crystal flat back, SS34, amethyst
- Magnetic clasp
- Chain- or flat-nose pliers, 2 pairs
- 2 twisted jump rings, large, copper

HOW TO MAKE IT

Place the metal clay on a texture plate, roll it out 6 cards thick, and then carefully remove the clay from the texture plate. Use a cookie cutter to cut out two large rectangles from the textured clay. As shown in photo A, use a cookie cutter to cut out a small rectangle centered inside each large rectangle. Let the metal clay dry.

A

As shown in photo B, make a centered hole on one thin edge of each rectangle with a craft knife.

B

Place the metal clay pieces between layers of activated coconut carbon in a firing container. Fire the clay in the kiln, following the manufacturer's instructions. Tumble the fired pieces until you're satisfied with their polish.

Determine what width of beaded strip will fit around the metal clay bar. Determine what length of beaded strip you need to fit your wrist.

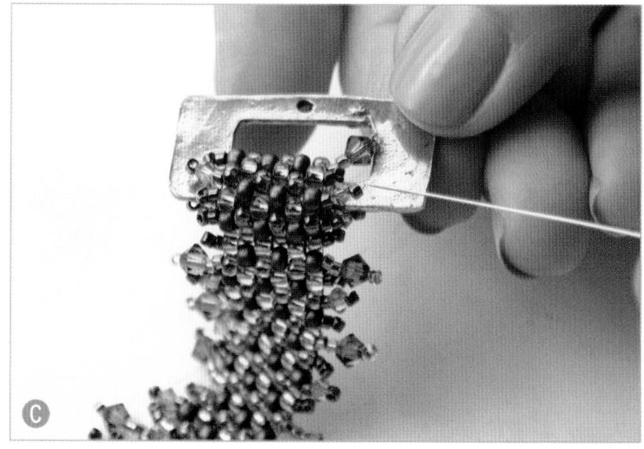

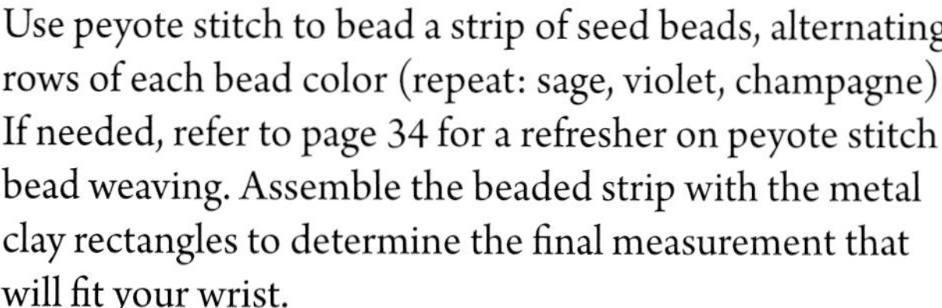

Use peyote stitch to bead a strip of seed beads, alternating rows of each bead color (repeat: sage, violet, champagne). If needed, refer to page 34 for a refresher on peyote stitch bead weaving. Assemble the beaded strip with the metal clay rectangles to determine the final measurement that will fit your wrist.

As shown in photo C, wrap one end of the beaded strip around the rectangle bar, and stitch to secure. Repeat this process on the opposite end of the strip.

Finish the strip by beading fringe down both edges of the bracelet in the following sequence. (All seed beads are size 15°.) Repeat this sequence as often as needed to finish the entire edge. Repeat on the second edge. (The fringe sequence was repeated 13 times per edge in my project.)

2 copper seed beads
copper seed bead, Colorado light topaz bicone, copper seed bead
2 copper seed beads
2 gold seed beads, amethyst bicone, gold seed bead

Mix the two-part epoxy. Glue the flat back amethyst crystal onto the magnetic clasp (photo D). Let the epoxy cure completely. Use a twisted jump ring to attach the magnetic toggle to one end of the bracelet. Attach the bar to the opposite end with a twisted jump ring.

Russian rhapsody herringbone lariat

I've had a long-standing love affair with Russian pendants. They're hand painted on black onyx by Russian artisans, and I drool over their vibrant colors and designs. The perfect way to display these stunning beauties is to attach them to a removable bail. For different looks, you can wrap the super long lariat around your neck a couple of times, tie it in a knot, or just let it hang down elegantly.

WHAT YOU NEED

- Metal clay toolbox, page 14
- Copper clay
- Cookie cutter, medium circle
- Bead tube
- Small marble or round bead
- Brown permanent marker
- Polishing pads
- Beading thread, 6 or 10 pound, dark color
- Beading needle
- Seed beads, size 8°, 1 gram each:
  - opaque matte gray
  - transparent light blue lined with copper
  - opalescent pink lined
  - metallic chrome blue
  - irridescent copper tube bead
  - opaque matte turquoise
  - opaque matte brown
  - transparent dark blue lined with copper
  - metallic chrome copper
- 6 crystal bicones, 3 mm, violet
- 2 crystal briolettes, 6 mm, copper
- 2 crystal briolettes, 6 mm, erinite
- Crystal briolette, 8 mm, copper
- Russian painted pendant*
- Head pin, gunmetal, 3 inches (7.6 cm)
- 2 eye pins, antique brass, 2 inches (5.1 cm)
- Crystal round, 4 mm, blue
- 4 crystal bicones, 4 mm, violet AB
- 8 crystal bicones, 4 mm, copper
- 24 head pins, antique brass, 2 inches (5.1 cm)
- 2 small jump rings, antique brass

*Available at www.Artbeads.com

HOW TO MAKE IT

Draw and cut out a 3-inch-long (7.6 cm) and 1-inch-wide (2.5 cm) strip of paper to use as a pattern for the metal clay bail. Taper one end of the pattern to a point. Place the copper clay on top of a texture plate, and roll it out 4 cards thick. Carefully remove the clay from the texture plate. Place the paper pattern on top of the clay, and cut around it with a needle tool to form the bail strip. Use the cookie cutter to cut out two circles. See photo A.

Wrap the clay bail strip around the bead tube with the tapered end on top, and let dry. Position the clay circles on top of the marble or round bead, and shape the clay to form a bead cap. Let dry. Using a craft knife, make centered holes in the top of the bead caps and in the tapered end of the bail as shown in photo B.

Place the bead caps and the bail in the activated coconut carbon. Fire the pieces in the kiln, following the manufacturer's instructions. Tumble the fired components until you're satisfied with their polish.

A

B

Russian rhapsody herringbone lariat

Add color to the bead caps and bail with a brown permanent marker. Use polishing pads to buff off the marker on the highest surfaces.

Stitch 46 inches (1.17 m) of tubular herringbone, alternating colors of seed beads in the following order. (For a refresher on the tubular herringbone stitch, see page 33.)

1 row opaque matte gray
1 row transparent light blue lined with copper
1 row opalescent pink lined
1 row metallic chrome blue
1 row irridescent copper tube bead
1 row opaque matte turquois
1 row opaque matte brown
1 row transparent dark blue lined with copper
1 row metallic chrome copper

String the following elements onto the longest head pin in this order: opalescent pink seed bead, erinite briolette, 8-mm copper briolette, Russian pendant, and erinite briolette. Make a simple open loop at the top of the head pin. Connect the head pin to the bail, and close the top loop. Slide the bail onto the tubular herringbone lariat.

At one end of the herringbone tube, stitch through opposite beads four to five times in each direction to build up a band of beading threads. Open the eye pin, slip the threads into the loop, and close the loop. String the bead cap and briolette onto the eye pin as shown in photo C. Finish off with a copper briolette and wrapped loop at the end. Repeat this step on the other end of the herringbone tube.

Using an assortment of seed beads and crystals, make 24 head pin dangles of varying lengths with a small loop at the top of each dangle. Connect 12 dangles to each bead cap loop with a jump ring.

crystal star bracelet

Make fringe bead stitched links and connect the lavish toggle with jump rings. Use crystal ABs for the crème de la crème in bling, and watch the design come full circle.

crystal star bracelet

WHAT YOU NEED

- Metal clay toolbox, page 14
- Copper clay
- Cookie cutters: large and small circles
- Beading needle, size 12°
- Beading thread, 6 pound, dark color
- Seed beads, size 15°, 0.5 gram, blue
- 43 crystal bicones, 4 mm, Montana 2AB
- Chain- or flat-nose pliers, 2 pairs
- Wire cutters
- 6 jump rings, large

HOW TO MAKE IT

Place the metal clay on top of a texture plate, and roll out the clay 5 cards thick. Carefully remove the clay from the texture plate. Use the larger cookie cutter to make two circles of textured metal clay. Place the smaller cookie cutter in the center of the larger metal clay circle. As shown in photo A, cut out and remove the interior circles to create metal clay rings. Let the rings dry.

Create a two-part textured toggle clasp—a bar and an off-centered ring—to match the metal clay rings. Let the toggle clasp dry completely, and then use a craft knife to make a hole in the thicker side of the toggle and in the center of the bar (photo B).

Arrange the dry metal clay pieces in a firing container between layers of activated coconut carbon. Fire them in the kiln, following the manufacturer's instructions. Tumble the fired pieces until you're satisfied with their polish.

Beading the Stars

Thread a needle with 1 yard (0.91 m) of beading thread, leaving a 6-inch (15.2 cm) tail.

A

B

Making the Stars

String six blue seed beads and five blue crystals, alternating the bead types and starting and ending with a seed bead. Shape the strung beads into a circle, and tie with a surgeon's knot. Pass the thread through the circle, and exit bead 3.

String three seed beads, one crystal, then three seed beeds. Skip the next crystal in the circle, and pass the thread through seed bead 5.

Continue around the entire circle, repeating this pattern (3 seed beads, 1 crystal, 3 seed beeds) passing the thread through seed beads 7, 9, 11, and 1, and exiting bead 3.

Pass through the next three seed beads and crystals, 13–16.

String one seed bead, one crystal, and one seed bead. Pass through the next crystal, bead 23. Continue around the circle, repeating this bead pattern, passing through beads 30, 37, 44, and 51, and exiting crystal 16.

Pass back through the outer circle of beads to tighten the circle. Take care not to pull too tightly or the circle will distort. Exit crystal 51.

Knot the thread to the thread between beads a few times, but do not cut the thread.

Making the Bail

Make a circle bail on each side of the beaded circle by stringing five beads onto the working thread in this order: one seed bead, one crystal, one seed bead, one crystal, one seed bead. Pass back through the second seed bead. Reinforce the bail by passing back through all the beads.

String six seed beads, pass back through the main seed bead, and pass back through all the seed beads again for reinforcement. Weave the thread through the beads, and tie off with knots.

Repeat "Making the Bail" to create a second circle bail on the other side of the circle.

Repeat "Making the Star" and "Making the Bail" to create a total of three stars with double bails.

Arrange the bracelet elements, inserting a metal clay ring between each beaded star. Attach the rings to the bails on the stars with jump rings. Attach the toggle bar to one end of the bracelet with a jump ring (photo D), and then attach the toggle to the other end in the same fashion.

C

D

ring around the rosy necklace

Texturize and patina to your heart's desire on this customizable necklace project. It's impossible to make a mistake, so don't be afraid to dive in and make it as lush as you like!

WHAT YOU NEED

- Metal clay toolbox, page 14
- Copper clay
- Bronze clay
- Cookie cutters: various size circles
- Gilders paste in Lilac, African Bronze, Patina
- 2 stiff brushes
- Soft buffing cloth
- Decoupage medium
- Beading wire, 1/55 inch (0.46 mm), copper
- Chain, 22 inches (55.9 mm)
- Crystal bicones, 4 mm, assorted colors (number varies according to how many rings you make)
- Seed beads, size 8°, assorted colors (number varies according to how many rings you make)
- Crimps (number varies according to how many rings you make)
- Crimping tool
- Wire cutter
- Chain- or flat-nose pliers, 2 pairs
- Toggle clasp
- 2 jump rings, large, copper

HOW TO MAKE IT

Place one kind of metal clay on top of a texture plate. Roll out the clay 6 cards thick. Place another texture plate on top of the clay, and roll it out 5 cards thick. This creates texture on both sides of the clay. Carefully remove the clay from the texture plate. Cut out clay circles, as many as you wish, in a variety of shapes and sizes. (The pictured project features 11 circles plus one for the toggle, some from copper clay and some from bronze.) Cut out a smaller circle in the center of each clay circle to form rings (photo A). Let dry.

To create a matching toggle clasp, cut out a toggle bar and let dry. Use a craft knife to make a hole in the center of the toggle bar and in one of the rings.

Place the metal clay pieces in a firing container between layers of activated coconut carbon. Position the container in the kiln, and fire the clay according to the manufacturer's instructions. Tumble the fired pieces until you're satisfied with their polish.

ring around the rosy necklace

Apply gilders paste to some of the fired rings with a stiff brush (photo B). (You can also use your finger to apply the paste.) Explore layering different colors of paste on the same ring. Let the rings sit for 24 hours.

Buff the excess color off the rings until you're happy with their luster finish. Seal each ring by brushing on a layer of decoupage medium. Let this topcoat dry completely.

Bead a variety of rings to intersperse with the metal clay ones on the necklace. The pictured project features 28 beaded rings, each one alternating 13 seed beads and 13 crystal beads. For each ring you make, string an alternating sequence of seed beads and crystal beads, finishing with one crimp bead. Form the beaded length into a circle, and crimp to secure. Repeat this process using a variety of seed beads and crystals as often as desired. Slip the beaded rings and the metal rings onto the chain in a random fashion as shown in photo C.

Once you're pleased with your masterpiece, attach the toggle and toggle bar to the chain ends with jump rings (photo D).

peyote cuff with metal leaves

Who doesn't love a touch of fringe playfully dangling around their wrist? Count me in! These tiny leaves and the focal piece are a blast to make and add movement to a basic peyote-stitched cuff.

peyote cuff with metal leaves

WHAT YOU NEED

- Metal clay toolbox, page 14
- Sterling silver metal clay
- Black permanent marker
- Polishing cloth
- Dapping block, optional
- Gilders paste (I used Pinotage)
- Cookie cutters: small flower and small leaf
- Beading thread, 6 or 10 pound, dark color
- Beading needle
- Seed beads, size 8°, 28 grams of each color: pink, dark green, mint green
- Seed beads, size 11°, 7.5 grams of each color: green, maroon, crystal
- Crystal bicones, 4 mm, erinite green
- 22 jump rings, 5 mm, black
- Two-part epoxy
- Flat back crystal, SS34, pink
- Two snaps

HOW TO MAKE IT

Roll out the metal clay 4 cards thick. Carve a flower shape from the clay by hand, and use a needle tool to stipple texture into the clay as shown in photo A. Make sure the flower shape has openings through which it can later be sewn onto the bracelet.

Place the leftover clay on a texture plate, roll it out 3 cards thick, and punch out a small flower shape. Roll out the leftover clay 2 cards thick, punch out 22 small leaves, and carve the veins freehand. Let the metal clay elements dry completely. Use a craft knife to make a centered hole at the wide end of each metal leaf.

Following the manufacturer's instructions, fire the sterling silver metal clay pieces in the kiln, and then fire a second time. Tumble the fired clay until you're satisfied with the polish.

Color the textured flower and leaves with a black permanent marker. Buff off the high surfaces with a polishing cloth. The black ink will stay in the crevices, darkening them for more definition. Optional: Use a dapping block to slightly dome the textured flower if desired.

Following the manufacturer's instructions, rub the gilders paste on the textured flower (photo B), let dry, and buff.

A

B

Beading the Bracelet

Measure around your wrist, and add a bit extra length to account for the overlap of the snap. Use the peyote stitch to create the bracelet band, alternating rows of size 8° mint green, pink, and dark green seed beads. (For a refresher on the peyote stitch, see page 34.) The pictured bracelet is 14 beads wide and 8 inches (20.3 cm) long.

Start trimming one edge of the bracelet with individual lengths of fringe in the following order. All seed beads used are size 11°.

2 maroon seed beads
3 green seed beads
2 maroon seed beads
3 green seed beads
2 maroon seed beads

Continue creating the trim by repeating this sequence approximately 11 times:

1 crystal seed bead, 1 bicone, 1 crystal seed bead
2 maroon seed beads
4 green seed beads (looped into next bead on edge)
2 maroon seed beads

To complete trimming the edge, repeat the initial sequence as follows:

2 maroon seed beads
3 green seed beads
2 maroon seed beads
3 green seed beads
2 maroon seed beads

Repeat the entire sequence on the opposite edge of the bracelet to create the trim.

As shown in photo C, use jump rings to attach a metal leaf to each green seed-bead loop along both edges of the bracelet.

Using two-part epoxy, glue the small flower on top of the textured flower shape and the flat back crystal on top of the flower (photo D). Let the epoxy fully cure.

Sew the flower onto the center of the cuff. Sew one half of the snaps onto opposite sides at each end of the bracelet.

C

D

wire lace crystal netting bracelet

This delicate yet durable bracelet shows off a touch of metallic wire lace — it's woven through the center of the design and coordinates with the ornate toggle. Your friends will want one in every color, please!

WHAT YOU NEED

- Metal clay toolbox, page 14
- Bronze clay
- Cookie cutters: medium, small, and extra small circles
- Bead stopper
- Beading thread, 6 or 10 pound, dark color
- Beading needle
- Seed beads, size 15°, 1 gram, antique gold
- 75 crystal bicones, 4 mm, Siam AB2X
- 37 crystal pearls, 3 mm, powder rose
- Wire lace, 3 mm, brass, 10 inches (25.4 cm) long
- Large-eye needle
- GS Hypo Cement
- 2 jump rings, copper, small

HOW TO MAKE IT

Place the metal clay on a texture plate, and roll out the clay 4 cards thick. Carefully remove the clay from the texture plate. Use a medium round cookie cutter to cut out a circle. Use the small and extra small round cookie cutters to cut out shapes inside the medium clay circle (photo A). Cut out a clay bar that is the length of the medium circle. Let all clay shapes completely dry.

Use a craft knife to make a hole through the center of the clay bar. Place the clay pieces between layers of activated coconut carbon inside a firing container. Fire them in the kiln, following the manufacturer's instructions. Tumble the pieces until you're satisfied with their polish.

A

wire lace crystal netting bracelet

Stitching the Bracelet

Put a bead stopper on the end of a 5-foot (1.5 m) length of thread, leaving a 4-inch (10.2 cm) tail.

String beads in the following order. (All seed beads are size 15° antique gold. All bicones are 4-mm crystals Siam AB2X.)

Seed bead A
Bicone A
Seed bead B
Bicone B
Seed bead C
Bicone C

Stitch through the A beads and the B beads.

String beads in the following order. (All seed beads are size 15° antique gold. All bicones are 4-mm crystals Siam AB2X.)

Seed bead D
Bicone D
Seed bead E
Bicone E
Seed bead F

Stitch up through bicone C, and pull snug into a circle.

Stitch through the D and E beads.

Flip over the bracelet.

B

C

Repeat the D, E, and F bead series until you've stitched 7 to 7½ inches (17.8 to 19.1 cm) depending on your wrist size.

Knot the thread. Stitch through the beads until you reach the first trio of seed beads.

Beginning at the end of one edge of the beaded strip, stitch a powder rose pearl between three antique gold seed beads. Repeat this process, stitching pearls down the entire row (photo B). Repeat this step on the opposite edge of the bracelet, ending up at the last bicone. Tie a knot in your thread.

String on nine antique gold seed beads and stitch through the next bicone, forming a loop. Secure the loop by stitching through the seed beads and end bicones two or three times. Knot the thread and stitch through the edge row until you reach the other end of the bracelet and come out at the last bicone.

String on nine antique gold seed beads and stitch through the next bicone to form a loop. Secure the loop by stitching through the seed beads and the end bicones two to three times.

Thread the wire lace through the large-eye needle. Stitch through the bicone at the end of the bracelet. Stitch under the next middle bicone. Come up over the next middle bicone. As shown in photo C, weave up and under the middle row of bicones, gently pulling the wire lace tight, until you reach the opposite end of the bracelet. Stitch through the last bicone.

Dab a bit of GS Hypo cement on both ends of the wire lace. Make certain the adhesive seeps into the bicones where the wire lace exits. Let dry. Clip off excess wire lace. As shown in photo D, attach the toggle clasp to the seed bead loops at the ends of the bracelet with jump rings.

triple strand bracelet with copper triangle beads

I based these triangle designs on the Batik Beauty fabric beads in my first book, *Fabulous Fabric Beads.* I wanted to re-explore a theme I originally created in fabric, but with metal clay this time. I give it a thumbs up!

WHAT YOU NEED

- Metal clay toolbox, page 14
- Copper clay
- Coffee stir straws
- Wire cutter
- Beading wire, bronze, 1⁄55 inch (0.46 mm), 30 inches (76.2 cm) long
- Bead stoppers, small
- Seed beads, size 11°, 1 gram: matte aqua lined with copper
- 25 crystal pearls, 3 mm, copper
- 10 fabric beads, ½ inch (1.3 cm), blues and greens
- 19 crystal bicones, 4 mm, copper
- 19 crystal bicones, 3 mm, indicolite
- 6 crimps
- Crimping pliers
- Chain- or flat-nose pliers, 2 pairs
- 2 eye pins
- Toggle clasp
- Bronze jump rings, 2 small, 1 large

HOW TO MAKE IT

Making the Metal Clay Beads

Place the metal clay on top of a texture plate, roll out the clay 4 cards thick, and carefully remove the clay from the texture plate. As shown in photo A, cut the clay into five triangles, each approximately 3 to 4 inches (7.6 to 10.2 cm) long by 1 inch (2.5 cm) wide. This measurement does not have to be exact—you may wish to vary the sizes of your beads.

A

triple strand bracelet with copper triangle beads

Carefully pick up one textured clay triangle. Starting at the wide end, roll the clay around a coffee stir straw (photo B). Make sure the textured side faces out and the tip of the triangle sticks to the bead body. Add a dab of slip to secure the connection if needed. Let the bead dry. Repeat this process with the rest of the clay triangles.

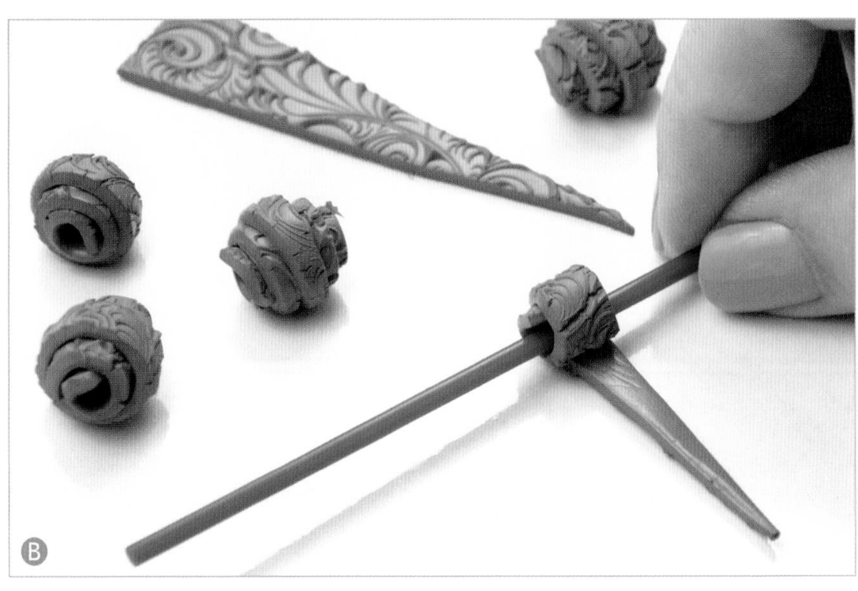
B

Place the metal clay beads in a firing container between layers of activated coconut carbon. Kiln-fire the clay, following the manufacturer's instructions. Tumble the pieces until you're satisfied with the polish.

Creating the Bracelet

Cut three strands of beading wire, each 10 inches (25.4 cm) long.

Strand One

Place a bead stopper at the end of one wire. String beads in this order:

seed bead
copper crystal
fabric bead
copper pearl
fabric bead
copper pearl
fabric bead
copper crystal
copper triangle bead
copper crystal
fabric bead
copper pearl
fabric bead
copper crystal
copper triangle bead
copper crystal
fabric bead
copper pearl
fabric bead
copper crystal
copper triangle bead
copper crystal
fabric bead
copper pearl
fabric bead
copper pearl
fabric bead
copper crystal
seed bead

Strand Two

Place a bead stopper on the end of a wire. String beads in this order:

3 seed beads
copper crystal
2 seed beads
copper crystal
2 seed beads
copper crystal
2 seed beads
copper crystal
2 seed beads

Slip the beading wire through the first triangle bead, and string:

2 seed beads
copper crystal
2 seed beads
copper crystal
2 seed beads
copper crystal

Slip the beading wire through the second triangle bead, and string:

2 seed beads
copper crystal
2 seed beads
copper crystal
2 seed beads
copper crystal
2 seed beads

Slip the beading wire through the third triangle bead, and string:

1 seed bead
copper crystal
2 seed beads
copper crystal
2 seed beads
copper crystal
2 seed beads
copper crystal
2 seed beads
copper crystal
3 seed beads

Strand Three
Place a bead stopper on the end of a wire. String beads in this order:

seed bead
copper pearl
indicolite crystal
copper pearl
indicolite crystal
copper pearl
indicolite crystal
copper pearl
indicolite crystal
copper pearl
indicolite crystal
copper pearl
seed bead

Slip the beading wire through the first triangle bead, and string:

seed bead
indicolite crystal
copper pearl
indicolite crystal
copper pearl
indicolite crystal
copper pearl
indicolite crystal
seed bead

Slip the beading wire through the second triangle bead, and string:

seed bead
indicolite crystal
copper pearl
indicolite crystal
copper pearl
indicolite crystal
copper pearl
indicolite crystal
copper pearl
seed bead

Slip the beading wire through the third triangle bead, and string:

seed bead
copper pearl
indicolite crystal
copper pearl
indicolite crystal
copper pearl
indicolite crystal
copper pearl
indicolite crystal
copper pearl
indicolite crystal
copper pearl
indicolite crystal
2 seed beads

NOTE

The number of seed beads on each strand can vary depending on the size of the other beads. Add or remove as many seed beads as needed to make each strand the same length.

Make a small loop at the end of each wire, and crimp the ends of the beading wires to secure. Slip all three wire loops onto an eye pin (photo C), and close the eye pin. Slide a triangle bead over the eye pin, and make a simple loop at the top of the bead. Repeat this step on the opposite ends of the three beading wires.

As shown in photo D, attach the toggle to one end of the bracelet with the large jump ring. Attach the toggle bar to the other end of the bracelet with two small jump rings.

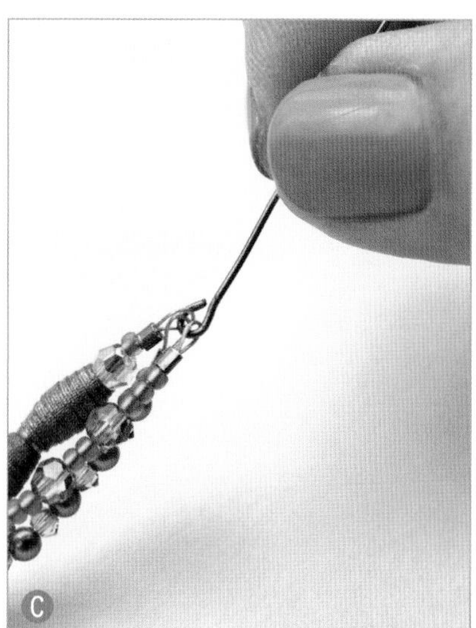
C

D

pet tags

Customized with a touch of bling and stamped with a special message, these tags for your pets are adorable!

WHAT YOU NEED

- Metal clay toolbox, page 14
- Copper clay
- Cookie cutters: heart, flower, bone, and square
- Quote stamp, optional
- Black permanent marker
- Polishing pad
- Two-part epoxy
- 2 flat back crystals, SS20, amethyst
- Lobster clasp
- Chain- or flat-nose pliers, 2 pairs
- Jump ring, large, copper

HOW TO MAKE IT

Place the metal clay on top of a texture plate. Roll out the clay to 4 cards thick. Carefully remove the clay from the texture plate. Use cookie cutters to cut out the dog bone, flower, heart, and square shapes (photo A). Stamp or write a quote on the clay square. Let all clay shapes dry.

Make a centered hole near the top edge of the bone. As shown in photo B, attach the clay embellishments to the bone with slip. Let the clay dry.

Place the metal clay in the firing container between layers of activated coconut carbon. Following the manufacturer's instructions, fire the clay in the kiln. Tumble the fired clay until you're happy with its polish.

As shown in photo C, color the recesses in the textured surface and the quote with a black permanent marker. Buff off the high points with a polishing pad. The black ink will stay in the crevices and darken the words for more definition and better readability.

Mix the two-part epoxy, and glue the flat back crystals onto the heart and flower shapes (photo D). Let cure. For the final touch, use a large jump ring to add the lobster clasp to the top of the tag.

A

B

C

D

caged crystal flower earrings

I love mixing metals in my jewelry designs. For these earrings, I made the large flowers copper and the small ones bronze. Remember to always fire the two metal clays separately. Once in a while, I sneak a very small, thin piece or two of copper in my bronze firings, but I can't ever be sure of the outcome. I've just been very lucky so far!

WHAT YOU NEED

- Metal clay toolbox, page 14
- Copper clay
- Bronze clay
- Cookie cutters: large, medium, and small flowers
- Black permanent marker
- Polishing pad
- Craft wire, black, 20 gauge, two 7-inch (17.8 cm) pieces, two 2-inch (5.1 cm) pieces
- Wire cutters
- Round-nose pliers
- Chain- or flat-nose pliers
- 2 crystals, each 16 x 14 mm, red cosmic
- 2 ear wires, black
- 6 jump rings, small, black
- 2 crystal briolettes, Colorado light topaz

HOW TO MAKE IT

Place the copper clay on top of a texture plate, roll it out 4 cards thick, and carefully remove the clay from the texture plate. Use a cookie cutter to cut out two large clay flowers. Cut a small flower out of the center of each large flower (photo A).

Place the bronze clay on top of a texture plate, roll it out 4 cards thick, and carefully remove the clay from the texture plate. Use a cookie cutter to cut out two medium clay flowers. Let the clay dry.

A

caged crystal flower earrings

Decide the orientation of both large copper flowers. Make sure a petal is at the top and bottom. Use a craft knife to make a centered hole through the top and bottom petals of the two large flowers. Make a centered hole near the top of both small bronze flowers.

Place the copper clay pieces in a firing container between layers of activated carbon. Fire the clay in the kiln, following the manufacturer's instructions. Tumble the fired pieces until you're satisfied with their polish.

Place the bronze clay pieces in a firing container between layers of activated carbon. Fire the clay in the kiln, following the manufacturer's instructions. Tumble the fired pieces until you're satisfied with their polish.

Color the metal flowers with a black permanent marker. Use a polishing pad to buff the ink off the high points of the texture.

Bend one 7-inch (17.8 cm) piece of wire in half. Using round-nose pliers, roll a loop at the end of the wire. Using chain- or flat-nose pliers, tightly coil the wire until you reach the bend in the center. Starting at the other wire end, make a loop and coil the wire in the opposite direction. You'll end up with an S-coil as shown in photo B. Repeat this process with the second 7-inch (17.8 cm) wire.

Stick the end of the round-nose pliers into the center of one wire coil. Poke up the wire until the coil looks like a little hat. Repeat for the second wire coil. Place a cosmic crystal in the middle of one of the wire "hats." Bend over the other "hat" on top of the crystal as shown in photo C. Gently shape the wire with your fingers to get the look you want. Repeat with the second wire coil and cosmic crystal.

B

C

Use round-nose pliers to make a small loop at the top of one 2-inch (5.1 cm) wire, creating an eye pin. Slide the wire through the caged crystal bead. Finish off by bending a second loop at the top of the crystal (photo D). Repeat this step with the second caged crystal.

Open the bottom loop in the eye pin under one crystal, add one small bronze flower, and close the loop. Repeat this process on the second crystal.

Open the loop above the crystal, feed the wire through the bottom hole in the large copper flower, and close the loop. Repeat this process on the second crystal.

Link three small, black jump rings together. Connect a crystal briolette to a jump ring at one end of the chain. Connect the ear wire through the hole at the top of the large copper flower and then through the top jump ring of the briolette chain. Repeat this step to make and attach the second embellished ear wire.

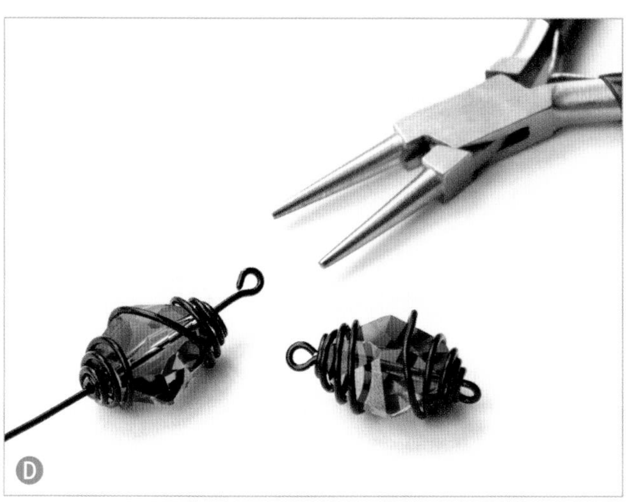

flower power necklace

The ever-popular Pandora-style beads inspired me to create these cute 3D flowers. There are many variations you can try, such as loading up the flower's edge with chatons or stacking them up to create your own mini garden. How enjoyable!

WHAT YOU NEED

- Metal clay toolbox, page 14
- Bronze clay
- Cookie cutters: small flower, large flower, and small circle
- Two-part epoxy
- 25 chatons, sized to fit indentations **after** firing, light blue, dark blue
- Beading wire, bronze, 1/55 inch (0.46 mm)
- 2 seed beads, size 8°, bronze
- 34 bicones, 4 mm, Colorado light topaz AB
- 26 twist bugle beads, 12 x 2 mm, blue
- 16 bicones, 4 mm, copper
- 20 rondelles, 6 mm, indicolite
- 2 crimps, bronze
- Crimping pliers
- 2 jump rings, bronze

HOW TO MAKE IT

Place the metal clay on top of a texture plate, and roll out the clay 12 cards thick. Place a second texture plate on top of the clay. Gently press the plate or roll it until the clay is 8 to 10 cards thick. Use a cookie cutter to cut five or six small flowers from the textured clay (photo A). (You only need three flowers, but you'll want extras to pick from for your final project.) Let the clay dry.

Create a hole in the middle of each flower by twirling the blade of a craft knife in a circular motion. Carve small, shallow indentations on the sides of each flower (photo B). (You'll glue chatons into these indentations later, after firing the clay.)

flower power necklace

Creating the Toggle

Place the metal clay on top of a texture plate, and roll it 4 cards thick. Carefully remove the clay from the texture plate. Use a cookie cutter to cut out a large clay flower. Make a hole in the center of the flower with the small circle cutter (photo C).

Use a craft knife to cut out a 1¼ x ¾-inch (3.2 x 1.9 cm) toggle bar. Let dry.

Make a hole through the center of one petal on the large flower and through the middle of the toggle bar. Carve small, shallow indentations in the center of each petal on the large flower and on the sides of hole in the toggle bar. (You'll glue chatons into these indentations later, after firing the clay.)

Place the metal pieces in the firing container between layers of activated coconut carbon. Fire the clay in the kiln, following the manufacturer's instructions. Tumble the fired clay pieces until you're satisfied with their polish.

Mix the two-part epoxy, and use it to adhere the chatons to the metal clay. Let the epoxy cure completely.

String the beads on the bronze beading wire in the following order:

> bronze seed bead

Repeat this sequence 13 times:

> Colorado light topaz bicone
> bugle bead
> Colorado light topaz bicone

Repeat this sequence eight times:

> indicolite rondelle
> copper bicone
> indicolite rondelle

Repeat this sequence three times:

> Colorado light topaz bicone
> bronze clay flower bead
> Colorado light topaz bicone
> indicolite rondelle

Repeat this sequence eight times:

> copper bicone
> indicolite rondelle

Repeat this sequence 13 times:

> Colorado light topaz bicone
> bugle bead
> Colorado light topaz bicone
> bronze seed bead

Crimp both ends of the beading wire, making a small loop at each end of the necklace. Attach the flower toggle and toggle bar to the ends of the necklace with jump rings.

tubular herringbone necklace with flower

Encasing my custom fabrics in resin was on my artistic bucket list. I checked that off and decided they would really pop in silver flower petal frames. And what better way to present the flower than on a gorgeous herringbone necklace? Done, done, and done!

tubular herringbone necklace with flower

WHAT YOU NEED

- Metal clay toolbox, page 14
- Silver clay
- Beading thread, 6 or 10 pound, dark color
- Seed beads, #8, 5 grams each color: black opaque picasso, terracotta gold marble luster, lilac gray, matt black
- Seed beads, #15, 1 gram black
- 240 crystal AB bicones, 4 mm
- Flat back crystal, SS34, copper
- Black permanent marker
- Polishing pads
- Beading needle
- Cookie cutters: large leaf, small leaf, large circle, and small circle
- Fabric, 6-inch (15.2 cm) square
- Decoupage medium, glossy
- Small paintbrush
- ICE resin
- Toothpicks
- Two-part epoxy
- Pin/pendant finding

HOW TO MAKE IT

Place the metal clay on top of a texture plate, and roll the clay out four-cards thick. Carefully remove the clay from the texture plate. Use the large leaf cookie cutter to cut out five large leaves. As shown in photo A, cut out the interior of each leaf with the small leaf cookie cutter.

Roll out a metal clay slab four-cards thick without any texture. Use cookie cutters to cut out a large clay circle and a small clay circle. Stipple dimples in the small circle with a needle tool. Let all metal clay components dry completely.

Place the dry clay pieces on the kiln shelf. Fire the clay according to the manufacturer's directions. Tumble the pieces until you are satisfied with their polish. Color the leaves and the small circle with a permanent black marker, and then buff off the excess color with a polishing pad.

A

B

Cut out five fabric pieces to fit inside the leaves, and seal each fabric piece with decoupage medium. Important: Make sure to seal the edges of the fabric as well as the front and back. This ensures that when the resin is applied, it won't seep into the fabric. If this does occur, the resin will turn the fabric very dark.

Adhere each leaf onto a piece of clear packing tape. Burnish the bottom of the leaves so the resin won't seep out from underneath the leaves. Place a sealed fabric piece in the center of each leaf as shown in photo B.

Mix the resin according to manufacturer's directions. Using a toothpick, carefully drop the resin into the interior of each leaf until it is full (photo C). Important: As tempting as it is to keep adding more resin, take your time and let each leaf self-settle so you don't overfill the interior. It's very difficult and messy to clean up an overfilled chamber—trust me on this! Let the resin-filled leaves fully cure for at least 24 hours, and then pull off the packing tape.

Mix the two-part epoxy according to the manufacturer's directions. Glue the leaves together forming a flower (photo D). Glue the large circle in the center of the flower. Glue the small circle in the center of the large circle, and glue the flat-back crystal in the center of the small circle. Let the epoxy completely dry. Turn over the flower, adhere the pin/pendant finding to the back with two-part epoxy, and let dry.

Following the series listed below, stitch 186 rows of tubular herringbone (14 total sets). Make one row of terracotta on each end of the tube.

2 rows black matte
2 rows terracotta
2 rows lilac gray
2 rows black opaque Picasso
2 rows terracotta
2 rows lilac gray
2 rows black opaque Picasso
2 rows terracotta
2 rows lilac gray
2 rows black opaque Picasso
2 rows black matte
1 row crystal
1 row black matte
1 row crystal

Add six fringe dangles to the ends of the tube, alternating six crystals with five black opaque picasso beads.

Pin the flower to the lariat, or wear the pin separately. You can also run a leather cord or chain through the pendant loop on the back of the pin.

C

D

butterfly earrings

I love incorporating symbolism into my jewelry designs and art whenever possible. Butterflies represent transformation and new beginnings, so these pretty pink dangles surround the wearer with positive vibes and blessings!

WHAT YOU NEED

- Metal clay toolbox, page 14
- Copper clay
- Cookie cutters: medium diamond and small teardrop
- Tissue blade, optional
- Metal patina paints, pink, orange
- Heat gun, optional
- Glaze
- Sanding block
- 4 head pins, copper, 1 inch (2.5 cm)
- 4 bicone crystals, 3 mm, fuchsia
- 2 bicone crystals, 4 mm, light Colorado topaz
- 2 crystal pearls, 4 mm, copper
- 2 bicone crystals, 3 mm, light Colorado topaz
- 2 crystal butterflies, 5 mm, fuchsia
- 2 bicone crystals, 4 mm, copper
- 2 baguette crystals, 8 mm, volcano
- 2 ear wires
- 2 twist jump rings, large, copper

HOW TO MAKE IT

Place the metal clay on a texture plate, and roll it 4 cards thick. Carefully remove the clay from the texture plate. Use a cookie cutter or a tissue blade to cut the textured metal clay into two diamond shapes the same size. As shown in photo A, cut out a centered teardrop shape from both clay diamonds, and let dry.

Make a hole near the top and bottom points of the clay diamonds. Place the metal clay in a firing container between layers of activated coconut carbon. Fire the metal clay in a kiln, following the manufacturer's instructions. Tumble the fired pieces until you're satisfied with the polish of the metal.

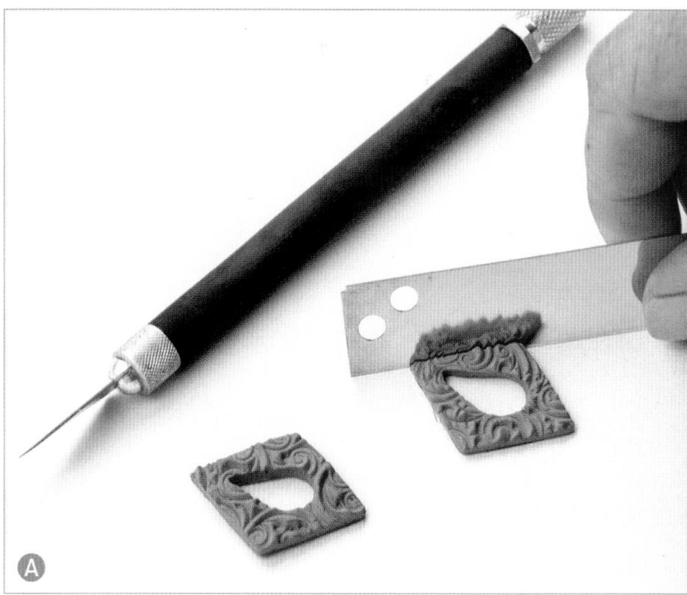
A

butterfly earrings

Brush pink and orange patina paints onto the fired metal as shown in photo B. Let the paints dry. (You can use a heat gun to speed up the drying process.) Apply a layer of glaze over the patina paints to seal them, and let dry.

Use a sanding block to remove the raised pattern on the clay so the metal shows through the patina (photo C).

B

String the following elements onto a copper head pin to make a dangle.

fuchsia crystal bicone
copper crystal pearl
Colorado light bicone crystal, 4 mm
fuchsia crystal bicone

Finish by making a small loop at the top of the head pin. Repeat this step to make a second dangle.

String the following elements onto a copper head pin to make a dangle.

copper crystal bicone
fuchsia crystal butterfly
Colorado light bicone crystal, 3 mm

Finish by making a small loop at the top of the head pin. Repeat this step to make a second dangle.

Slip the baguette crystal onto the ear wire as shown in photo D. Use a jump ring to attach the metal clay diamond and pearl dangle to the baguette. Attach the other dangle to the bottom hole of the metal clay diamond. Repeat this step to assemble the second earring.

C

D

five strand necklace with fabric beads

This was one of my favorite projects to create for the book. Metal clay bead frames and caps really add interest and depth to the overall assemblage. The featured mosaic crystal gives the piece an intriguing touch.

five strand necklace with fabric beads

WHAT YOU NEED

- Metal clay toolbox, page 14
- Copper clay
- Cookie cutters: large square, medium square, and small circle
- Bead reamer or drill bit
- Texture stick
- Polymer clay balls or large wooden beads
- 10 bead stoppers
- Beading wire, black, 1⁄55 inch (0.46 mm), six 15-inch (38.1 cm) strands
- Wire cutters

Strand 1

- 32 seed beads, size 6°, bronze
- 16 bicones, 4 mm, erinite green
- 8 beads, 18 mm, crystal golden shadow graphic
- 7 bicones, 8 mm, pacific opal

Strand 2

- 36 seed beads, size 6°, seafoam
- 37 seed beads, size 11°, copper metallic
- 4 rondelles, 6 mm, bronze
- 2 rondelles, 6 mm, purple velvet
- 5 resin nuggets, dark purple
- 4 resin nuggets, light purple
- 4 helix crystals, 8 mm

Strand 3

- 99 seed beads, size 8°, dark green
- 100 seed beads, size 11°, copper metallic

Strand 4

- 6 seed beads, size 11°, copper metallic
- 16 crystal bicones, 4 mm, light Colorado topaz
- 8 crystal rondelles, 6 mm, erinite green
- 14 crystal pearls, 8 mm, powder green
- 7 silk beads, 1⁄2 inch (1.3 cm), green

Strand 5

- 20 round crystals, 4 mm, jet AB
- 18 square seed beads, 4 mm, light purple
- 16 square seed beads, 4 mm, dark purple
- 4 crystal rondelles, 16 mm, copper
- 4 crystal rounds, 12 mm, purple velvet
- 1 rondelle, 16 mm, marbled sea green
- 10 crimps, copper
- Crimping tool
- Round-nose pliers
- Chain-nose pliers
- 2 eye pins, 2 inches (5.1 cm), antique brass
- 2 chains, each 3 inches (7.6 cm) long, antique copper
- Clasp, antique copper
- 4 jump rings, 5 mm, antique copper

HOW TO MAKE IT

Creating the Metal Clay Components

Place the copper clay on top of a texture plate. Roll out the clay 16 cards thick. Carefully remove the textured clay from the plate. Use a cutter to create a large metal clay square. Cut out a smaller square in the center of the large square, creating a frame, and let dry.

Cut out two small circles with cookie cutters. Shape one of the clay circles around the texture stick to create a bead cone. As shown in photo A, gently press the clay onto a texture plate. Repeat this process with the second clay circle.

A

Place the copper clay on top of a texture plate, and roll out the clay 4 cards thick. Carefully remove the clay from the plate. Cut out eight textured-clay circles with a cookie cutter. Shape the clay circles on top of the polymer clay balls or large wooden beads (photo B), and let dry. These are the bead caps.

As shown in photo C, make a centered hole through one side of the frame. Make the hole parallel rather than perpendicular to the clay surfaces. Use a craft knife to make a centered hole in each bead cap and bead cone.

Place the clay pieces in a firing container between layers of activated coconut carbon. Kiln-fire the clay, following the manufacturer's instructions. Tumble the fired clay pieces until you're satisfied with their polish.

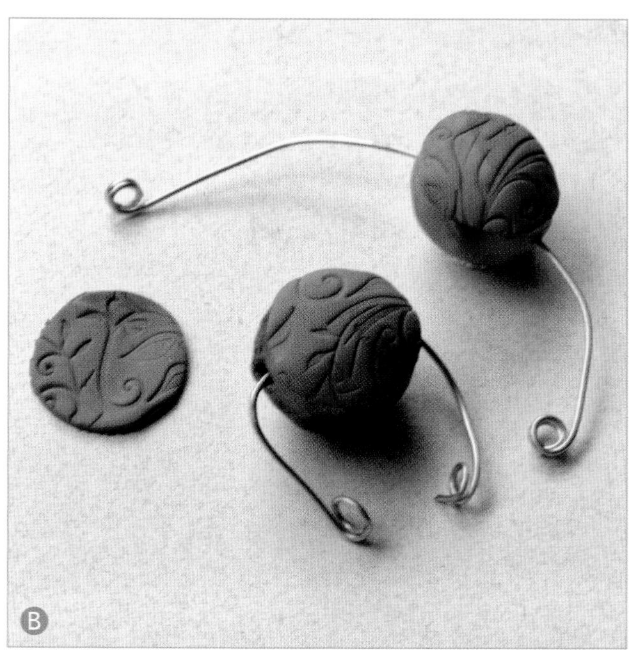

B

C

five strand necklace with fabric beads

Beading the Strands

Place a bead stopper on the end of one 15-inch (38.1 cm) strand of beading wire. To create strand 1, string beads onto the wire in the following order.

String this sequence of beads seven times:

bronze seed bead
erinite bicone
bronze seed bead
graphic bead
bronze seed bead
erinite bicone
bronze seed bead
pacific opal bicone

Complete the strand by stringing beads in this order:

bronze seed bead
erinite bicone
bronze seed bead
graphic bead
bronze seed bead
erinite bicone
bronze seed bead

Place a bead stopper on the end of a 15-inch (38.1 cm) strand of beading wire. To create strand 2, string beads onto the wire in the following order.

seafoam seed bead
copper metallic seed bead
seafoam seed bead
copper metallic seed bead
seafoam seed bead
copper metallic seed bead
seafoam seed bead
copper metallic seed bead
bronze rondelle
copper metallic seed bead
seafoam seed bead
copper metallic seed bead
seafoam seed bead
copper metallic seed bead
purple rondelle
copper metallic seed bead
seafoam seed bead
copper metallic seed bead
seafoam seed bead
dark purple resin nugget
seafoam seed bead
copper metallic seed bead
seafoam seed bead
copper metallic seed bead
bronze rondelle
copper metallic seed bead
seafoam seed bead
light purple resin nugget
seafoam seed bead
copper metallic seed bead
seafoam seed bead
copper metallic seed bead
helix crystal
copper metallic seed bead
seafoam seed bead
dark purple resin nugget
seafoam seed bead
light purple resin nugget
seafoam seed bead
copper metallic seed bead
helix crystal
copper metallic seed bead
seafoam seed bead
copper metallic seed bead
seafoam seed bead
dark purple resin nugget
seafoam seed bead
copper metallic seed bead
seafoam seed bead
copper metallic seed bead
helix crystal
copper metallic seed bead
seafoam seed bead
light purple resin nugget
seafoam seed bead
dark purple resin nugget
seafoam seed bead
copper metallic seed bead
helix crystal
copper metallic seed bead
seafoam seed bead
copper metallic seed bead
seafoam seed bead
light purple resin nugget
seafoam seed bead
copper metallic seed bead
bronze rondelle
copper metallic seed bead
seafoam seed bead
copper metallic seed bead
seafoam seed bead
dark purple resin nugget
seafoam seed bead
copper metallic seed bead
seafoam seed bead
copper metallic seed bead
purple rondelle
copper metallic seed bead
seafoam seed bead
copper metallic seed bead
seafoam seed bead
bronze rondelle
copper metallic seed bead
seafoam seed bead
copper metallic seed bead
seafoam seed bead
copper metallic seed bead
seafoam seed bead
copper metallic seed bead
seafoam seed bead

Place a bead stopper on the end of a 15-inch (38.1 cm) strand of beading wire. To create strand 3, string only seed beads onto the wire, alternating 99 dark green seed beads with 100 copper metallic seed beads.

Place a bead stopper on the end of a 15-inch (38.1 cm) strand of beading wire. To create strand 4, string beads onto the wire in the following order.

3 copper metallic seed beads

Repeat this sequence seven times:

light Colorado topaz crystal bicone
erinite crystal rondelle
light Colorado topaz crystal bicone
crystal powder green pearl
silk bead
crystal powder green pearl

String these beads to complete the strand:

light Colorado topaz crystal bicone
erinite crystal rondelle
light Colorado topaz crystal bicone
3 copper metallic seed beads

Place a bead stopper on the end of a 15-inch (38.1 cm) strand of beading wire. To create strand 5, string beads onto the wire in the following order.

jet AB round crystal
light purple square seed bead
dark purple square seed bead
light purple square seed bead
dark purple square seed bead
light purple square seed bead
jet AB round crystal
copper clay bead cap
copper rondelle
copper clay bead cap
jet AB round crystal
dark purple square seed bead
light purple square seed bead
dark purple square seed bead
light purple square seed bead
jet AB round crystal
purple crystal round
jet AB round crystal
dark purple square seed bead
light purple square seed bead
dark purple square seed bead
light purple square seed bead
jet AB round crystal
copper clay bead cap

five strand necklace with fabric beads

copper rondelle
copper clay bead cap
jet AB round crystal
dark purple square seed bead
light purple square seed bead
dark purple square seed bead
light purple square seed bead
jet AB round crystal
purple crystal round
jet AB round crystal
copper clay bead frame
jet AB round crystal
marbled sea green crystal rondelle
jet AB round crystal
copper clay bead frame
jet AB round crystal
purple crystal round
jet AB round crystal
light purple square seed bead
dark purple square seed bead
light purple square seed bead
dark purple square seed bead
jet AB round crystal
copper clay bead cap
copper rondelle
copper clay bead cap
jet AB round crystal
light purple square seed bead
dark purple square seed bead
light purple square seed bead
dark purple square seed bead
jet AB round crystal
purple crystal round
jet AB round crystal
light purple square seed bead
dark purple square seed bead
light purple square seed bead
dark purple square seed bead

D

jet AB round crystal
copper clay bead cap
copper rondelle
copper clay bead cap
jet AB round crystal
light purple square seed bead
dark purple square seed bead
light purple square seed bead
dark purple square seed bead
light purple square seed bead
jet AB round crystal

Make adjustments to each bead strand as needed so they're the same length. Crimp both ends of each bead strand, leaving a small loop. Open an eye pin, insert the five wire loops from one end, and close the eye pin. Repeat this process on the opposite ends of the necklace strands.

Thread a copper bead cone onto the eye pin, and make a wrapped loop at the top of the cone. Repeat with the opposite end as shown in photo D. Attach one length of chain to each bead cone with a jump ring. Attach one clasp element to each end of the chain with a jump ring.

starburst bracelet

I love using Swarovski sew-on components in my jewelry and wanted to feature the starburst with a silver stamped medallion and toggle. Add a dash of neon pearls to pop the look even more, and you end up with this beauty.

starburst bracelet

WHAT YOU NEED

Metal clay toolbox, page 14
Silver clay
Cookie cutters: circle and oval
Steel bench block
Stamp or punch, sunburst
Chasing hammer
Metal hole-punch pliers
Black permanent marker
Polishing pads
Beading wire, black, 1/52 inch (0.48 mm)
Wire cutters
20 bead stoppers
20 crystal rondelles, 3 mm, greige
18 crystal bicones, 3 mm, rose
20 seed beads, size 15°, clear
10 crystal bicones, 4 mm, light rose
8 crystal bicones, 4 mm, dark rose
18 seed beads, size 15°, silver
6 crystal pearls, 4 mm, red coral
6 crystal pearls, 4 mm, coral
6 crystal pearls, 4 mm, pink coral
16 crystal butterflies, 6 mm, golden shadow
14 crystal bicones, 3 mm, padparadscha
10 crystal rounds, 4 mm, sunflower
18 seed beads, size 15°, pink
10 bicones, 4 mm, fuchsia AB2X
20 crimps, black matte
Crimping tool
20 jump rings, black, 5 mm
Swarovski filigree, 20 mm
Two-part epoxy
Chain- or flat-nose pliers, 2 pairs

HOW TO MAKE IT

Place the metal clay on a texture plate, and roll out the clay 4 cards thick. Carefully remove the clay from the texture plate. Cut out a circle of textured clay with the cookie cutter. Cut the clay circle in half, and then cut out a half-moon shape in the center of each half circle. Cut a toggle bar from the textured clay to fit through one of the half circles.

Roll out more metal clay 4 cards thick, and use a cookie cutter to cut out an oval shape. Let all clay components dry completely.

As shown in photo A, create five equally spaced holes in the straight section of each half circle. On only one half circle, make a centered hole near the top of the curved portion. Make a hole in the middle of the toggle bar.

A

B

C

Place the metal clay pieces on the kiln shelf, and fire them according to the manufacturer's instructions. Tumble the fired pieces until you're satisfied with the polish. Place the solid metal oval on the steel bench block. Using the sunburst punch and chasing hammer, randomly hammer designs on the oval as shown in photo B.

Use the metal hole-punch pliers to punch out three equally spaced holes near the narrow ends of the oval (photo C). Color the toggle bar, the half circles, and the oval with a black permanent marker. Buff off the excess ink with polishing pads.

Cut 10 pieces of beading wire, each 4 inches (10.2 cm) long. Place a bead stopper on the end of each wire.

String beads in the following order, and then place a bead stopper at the end of each beaded strand.

Strands 1 & 2

Repeat this pattern 9 times:

greige crystal rondelle
rose crystal bicone

String one greige crystal rondelle to complete the strand.

Strands 3 & 4

Repeat this pattern four times:

clear seed bead
light rose crystal bicone
clear seed bead
dark rose crystal bicone

To complete the strand string:

clear seed bead
light rose crystal bicone
clear seed bead

Strands 5 & 6

Repeat this pattern three times:

silver seed bead
red coral crystal pearl
silver seed bead
pink coral crystal pearl
silver seed bead
coral crystal pearl

Strands 7 & 8

Repeat this pattern 7 times:

golden shadow crystal butterfly
padparadscha crystal bicone

String one golden shadow crystal butterfly to complete the strand.

starburst bracelet

Strands 9 & 10

Repeat this pattern four times:

> sunflower crystal round
> pink seed bead
> fuchsia AB2X bicone
> pink seed bead

To complete the strand string:

> sunflower crystal round
> pink seed bead
> fuchsia AB2X bicone

Adjust each beaded strand as needed so they're the same length. Crimp both ends of each strand, leaving a small loop.

Feed the looped ends of strand 1 and strand 3 onto a jump ring, and connect the jump ring to the bottom hole on the left side of the silver oval.

Feed the looped end of strand 5 onto a jump ring, and connect the jump ring to the middle hole on the left side of the silver oval.

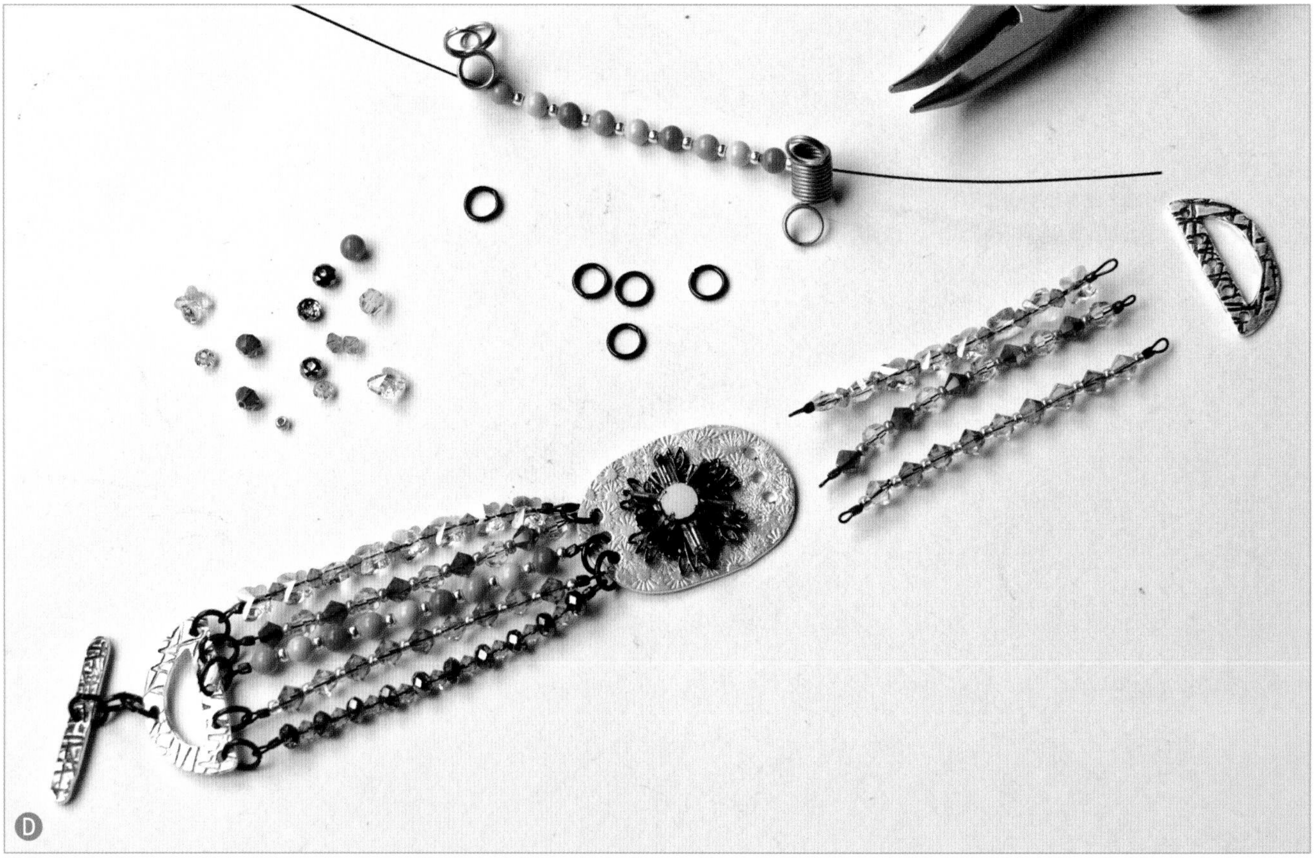

Feed the looped ends of strand 7 and strand 9 onto a jump ring, and connect the jump ring to the top hole on the left side of the silver oval.

Feed a jump ring on the opposite end of every beaded strand. Connect each ring through a hole in the metal clay half circle in this order, top to bottom: strand 7, strand 9, strand 5, strand 3, strand 1.

Repeat this process to attach the matching strands to the right side of the oval (photo D).

Attach the toggle bar to the half circle with four linked jump rings. Glue the filigree onto the silver oval with two-part epoxy. Let the epoxy fully cure.

dream necklace

I love including inspirational words in my jewelry designs. Pick your own special word to give a personal touch to your creation.

WHAT YOU NEED

- Metal clay toolbox, page 14
- Copper clay
- Cookie cutters: medium, small, and extra small circles
- Word stamp, optional
- Black permanent marker
- Polishing pads
- Gilders paste
- Stiff brush
- Decoupage medium
- 3 crystal rounds, 6 mm, copper
- 4 head pins
- Chain, ½ inch (1.3 cm), antique copper
- 4 jump rings, small
- Beading wire, 1/55 inch (0.46 mm), 25 inches (63.5 cm) long
- Wire cutter
- Crimping pliers
- 2 crimps, copper
- 16 crystal bicones, 4 mm, olivine
- 12 crystal pearls, 4 mm, platinum
- 6 triangle beads (see page 76, Triple Strand Bracelet, for instructions on making triangle beads)
- 2 fabric beads, ½ inch (1.3 cm), green
- 10 seed beads, size 11°, brown matte
- 10 flower spacers, copper
- 4 cosmic crystals, 12 x 11 mm, crystal bronze
- 8 crystal bicones, 4 mm, light Colorado topaz
- 18 crystal bicones, 3 mm, copper
- 4 fabric beads, 1 inch (2.5 cm), green
- 4 crystal pearls, 6 mm, antique brass
- 4 crystal pearls, 3 mm, platinum
- Chain, 16 inches (40.6 cm), antique copper
- 2 chains, 2 inches (5.1 cm) each, antique copper
- Jump ring, medium
- Jump ring, large twist, antique copper
- 3 eye pins
- 2 crystal pearls, 4 mm, antique brass
- 1 crystal bicone, 6 mm, khaki
- 2 crystal pearls, 3 mm, antique brass
- Chain- or flat-nose pliers, 2 pairs
- Round-nose pliers

HOW TO MAKE IT

Place the metal clay on top of a texture plate, and roll the clay 4 cards thick. Carefully remove the clay from the texture plate. As shown in photo A, cut out a large square pendant from the textured metal clay. Cut a diamond shape out of the square clay pendant. If desired, cut out a tag for a word stamp. Cut out a medium circle for the toggle clasp. Cut an off-centered small circle out of the interior of the medium circle and then a very small circle out of the wide part of the circle's edge. Cut out a toggle bar. Let all of these metal clay pieces completely dry.

As shown in photo B, attach the tag (if using) to the large square using lots of slip, and let dry.

A

Use a craft knife to drill one hole in the center of the toggle bar, and near each of the four corners of the large square.

Place the metal clay pieces between layers of activated coconut carbon inside a firing container. Fire the clay in the kiln, following the manufacturer's instructions. Tumble the pieces until you're happy with their polish.

B

Optional: Color the stamped word on the tag with a black permanent marker, and buff off excess ink with a polishing pad. (The black ink stays in the recesses and darkens the word for better visibility.)

dream necklace

Apply gilders paste to the pendant and the toggle with a stiff brush as shown in photo C. (Alternately, you can apply the paste with your finger.) Let the pendant and toggle sit for 24 hours, and then buff off the excess paste until you're happy with the luster finish. Seal the patina with a layer of decoupage medium, and let dry completely.

String the following beads onto the wire, and then crimp both ends, leaving a small loop at the top of the wire:

olivine crystal bicone, 4 mm
copper crystal round
platinum crystal pearl, 4 mm
triangle bead
platinum crystal pearl, 4 mm
olivine crystal bicone, 4 mm
fabric bead, 1/2 inch (1.3 cm)
olivine crystal bicone, 4 mm
brown seed bead
copper flower spacer
crystal bronze cosmic crystal
copper flower spacer
light Colorado topaz bicone
fabric bead, 1 inch (2.5 cm)
light Colorado topaz bicone
brown seed bead
platinum crystal pearl, 4 mm
triangle bead
platinum crystal pearl, 4 mm
brown seed bead
olivine crystal bicone
copper crystal bicone, 3 mm
platinum crystal pearl, 6 mm
copper crystal bicone, 3 mm
olivine crystal bicone
copper crystal bicone, 3 mm
copper flower spacer
crystal bronze cosmic crystal
copper flower spacer
copper crystal bicone, 3 mm
light Colorado topaz bicone
fabric bead, 1 inch (2.5 cm)
light Colorado topaz bicone
brown seed bead
platinum crystal pearl, 4 mm
triangle bead
platinum crystal pearl, 4 mm
brown seed bead
olivine crystal bicone
antique brass crystal pearl, 6 mm
olivine crystal bicone
4 platinum crystal pearls, 3 mm
olivine crystal bicone
antique brass crystal pearl, 6 mm
olivine crystal bicone
brown seed bead
platinum crystal pearl, 4 mm
triangle bead
platinum crystal pearl, 4 mm
brown seed bead

light Colorado topaz bicone
fabric bead, 1 inch (2.5 cm)
light Colorado topaz bicone
copper crystal bicone, 3 mm
copper flower spacer
crystal bronze cosmic crystal
copper flower spacer
copper crystal bicone, 3 mm
olivine crystal bicone
copper crystal bicone, 3 mm
antique brass crystal pearl, 6 mm
copper crystal bicone, 3 mm
olivine crystal bicone
brown seed bead
platinum crystal pearl, 4 mm
triangle bead
platinum crystal pearl, 4 mm
brown seed bead
light Colorado topaz bicone
fabric bead, 1 inch (2.5 cm)
light Colorado topaz bicone
copper crystal bicone, 3 mm
copper flower spacer
crystal bronze cosmic crystal
copper flower spacer
copper crystal bicone, 3 mm
brown seed bead
olivine crystal bicone, 4 mm
fabric bead, ½ inch (1.3 cm)
olivine crystal bicone, 4 mm
platinum crystal pearl, 4 mm
triangle bead
platinum crystal pearl, 4 mm
copper crystal round
olivine crystal bicone, 4 mm

dream necklace

Attach the loop at one end of the beaded necklace, one end of one short chain, and one end of the medium chain with a small jump ring. Attach the loop on the opposite side of the beaded necklace, one end of the second short chain, and the remaining end of the medium chain with a small jump ring.

Attach one remaining end of short chain to the toggle with a medium jump ring. Attach the toggle bar to the other chain end with a medium jump ring.

String a 6-mm copper round crystal onto a head pin. Make a wrapped loop, attaching the head pin to the ½-inch (1.3 cm) chain. Add a small jump ring to the other end of the chain.

Use the large jump ring to attach the metal clay pendant and the copper crystal chain dangle to the center of the necklace.

String beads onto an eye pin in this order to make a dangle:

copper crystal bicone, 3 mm
antique brass crystal pearl, 4 mm
khaki crystal bicone
antique brass crystal pearl, 3 mm
copper crystal bicone, 3 mm

Repeat this pattern with a second eye pin to make a second dangle. Make a simple loop at the top of each eye pin, and attach one dangle to the holes on the sides of the pendant.

To make the center dangle, string beads onto an eye pin in this order:

copper crystal bicone, 3 mm
olivine crystal bicone, 4 mm
copper flower spacer
large briolette
copper flower spacer
olivine crystal bicone, 4 mm
copper crystal bicone, 3 mm

As shown in photo D, finish the eye pin with a simple loop at the top, and attach the dangle to the center hole at the bottom of the pendant.

peyote stitch buckle bracelet

A timeless design, this peyote stitch bracelet lets you incorporate all your fave seed bead colors. The crystal edging adds just the right touch of sparkle to rock your jeans or dress up for happy hour. Make a longer version for a belt!

WHAT YOU NEED

- Metal clay toolbox, page 14
- Bronze clay
- Cookie cutters: large circle and small circle
- Beading needle
- Beading thread, 6 or 10 pound, dark color
- Seed beads, size 8°, 1 gram each color: blue matt, sea foam lined, amber lined
- Seed beads, size 15°, 1 gram, blue
- 68 light Colorado topaz crystal bicones, 4 mm
- Large snap

HOW TO MAKE IT

Place the clay on top of a texture plate, and roll it out 6 cards thick. Carefully remove the clay from the texture plate. Use a cookie cutter to cut out a large circle of textured clay. Cut out a medium circle from the center of the large circle of textured clay. You will end up with a large ring as shown in photo A.

Cut out a rectangle from the textured clay that is as long as the diameter of the large clay circle. Attach the rectangle to the back of the circle with slip (photo B), and let dry completely.

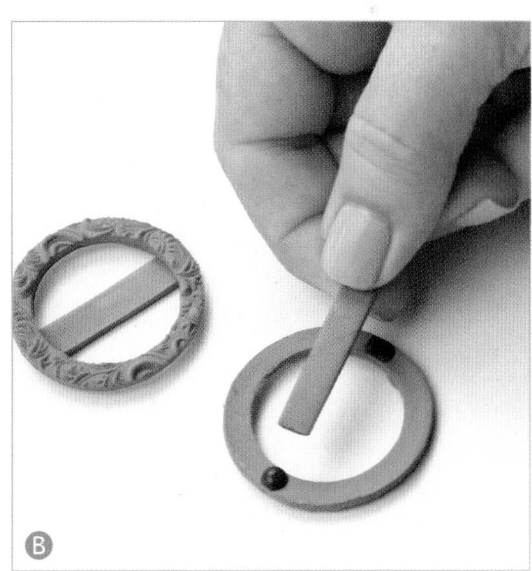

Place the metal clay piece in the firing container between layers of activated coconut carbon, and fire it in the kiln according to the manufacturer's directions. Tumble the fired metal clay until you're satisfied with its polish.

peyote stitch buckle bracelet

Measure around your wrist, and add a bit extra length to account for the overlap of the snap. Use peyote stitch to create the bracelet band, alternating rows of size 8° blue matt, sea foam lined, and amber lined seed beads. (For a refresher on the peyote stitch, see page 34.) The pictured bracelet is 10 beads wide and 8 inches (20.3 cm) long. Feed the beaded band through the metal clay buckle as shown in Photo C.

Trim the edges of the bracelet by stitching a blue seed bead (size 11°), a light Colorado topaz crystal bicone, and a second blue seed bead between each pair of beads along the long edge. To trim the ends of the bracelet, stitch two blue seed beads (size 11°) between each pair of beads. As shown in photo D, sew one half of the large snap onto opposite sides at each end of the bracelet.

C

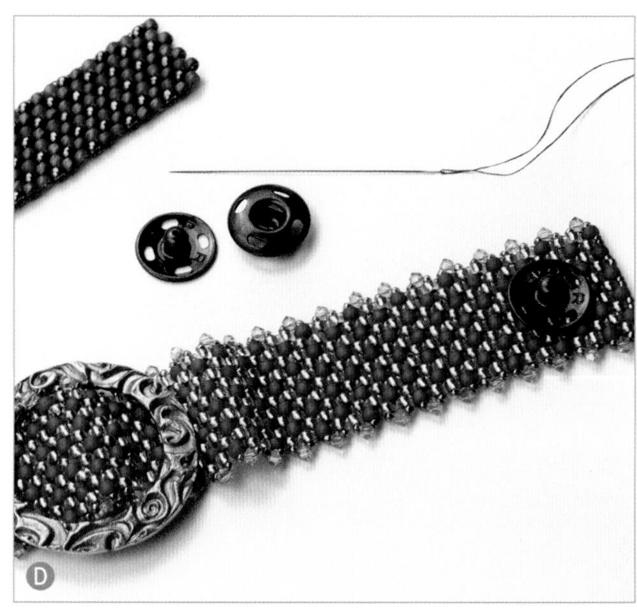

D

triple dangle earrings

Have fun mixing and matching crystal colors and fabric beads with chain for an unexpected effect in this simple project.

triple dangle earrings

WHAT YOU NEED

- Metal clay toolbox, page 14
- Copper clay
- Cookie cutters: large circle, medium circle, and small leaf
- Metal patina paints: amethyst, pink, dark blue
- Heat gun, optional
- Glaze
- Sanding block
- Black permanent marker
- Polishing pad
- 4 bicone crystals, 3 mm, amethyst
- 4 bicone crystals, 4 mm, violet AB
- 2 fabric beads, 1 inch (2.54 cm)
- 2 eye pins, copper, 2 inches (5.1 cm)
- 2 jump rings, small, purple
- 4 short chains, each ½ inch (1.3 cm) long
- 2 briolettes, 6 mm, amethyst AB
- 2 head pins, copper
- 2 short chains, each 1 inch (2.54 cm) long
- 4 jump rings, medium, copper
- 2 ear wires
- 2 seed beads, size 11°, purple
- 2 ear nuts

HOW TO MAKE IT

Place the copper clay on top of a texture plate. Roll out the clay 4 cards thick. Carefully remove the clay from the texture plate. Cut out two large clay circles. As shown in photo A, cut out a small circle from the interior of a large clay circle, closer to one edge. Repeat for the second clay circle. Cut out two small metal clay leaves. Let the metal clay elements dry completely.

Make a centered hole at the top of each large metal clay circle. Make three equidistant holes at the bottom of each circle. Make a hole near one end of each leaf charm.

Place the metal clay pieces in the firing container between layers of activated coconut carbon. Kiln-fire the metal clay, following the manufacturer's instructions. Tumble the fired pieces until you're satisfied with the polish.

As shown in photo B, apply amethyst and pink patina paints to the metal components with a brush. Let the patina paints completely dry. (You can use a heat gun to speed up the drying process.)

Mix one drop of dark blue patina with three drops of glaze. Brush a thin layer of this translucent wash onto the metal elements (photo C), and let dry.

Use a sanding block with gentle pressure to remove the raised pattern of the clay so the metal shows through the patina (photo D).

Darken the texture on the two leaf charms with a black permanent marker. Buff off excess ink with a polishing pad.

Make two long beaded dangles by stringing the following elements onto two copper eye pins:

amethyst bicone, 3 mm
violet AB bicone, 4 mm
fabric bead
violet AB bicone, 4 mm
amethyst bicone, 3 mm

Finish each dangle by making a small loop at the top and attaching it to the center hole at the bottom of each large metal circle. Add a leaf charm to the bottom of each eye pin using a purple jump ring.

Use medium jump rings to add a short chain to one empty hole and a longer chain to the other empty hole at the bottom of the large circles. Place each briolette on a head pin and form a wrapped loop, attaching each to the remaining $\frac{1}{2}$-inch (1.3 cm) chains. Open an ear wire loop, add a large circle and a briolette chain, and close the ear wire. Repeat this for the second earring. Slip a purple seed bead onto each ear wire.

cupcake charm bracelet with earrings

Take a few seed beads, a dash of silver, and cupcakes (of course), and you end up with this whimsical bracelet and earring set. Since Cupcake is my nickname, I feel obliged to indulge every chance I get! Enjoy, calorie free!

WHAT YOU NEED

- Metal clay toolbox, page 14
- Silver clay
- Small cookie cutters: leaf, flower, dragonfly, and heart
- Large cookie cutters: cupcake and circle
- Carving tool
- Metal hole-punch pliers
- Chasing hammer
- Steel bench block
- Heart stamp
- Black permanent marker
- Polishing pads
- Two-part epoxy
- 10 flat back crystals, small, pink
- 5 chatons, small, green
- 13 chatons, small, pink
- Pink cup chain, to fit finished cupcake charms
- 10 twist jump rings, 10 mm, gunmetal
- 17 jump rings, 8 mm, black
- 9 jump rings, 5 mm, black
- Black chain, 7½ inches (19.1 cm), cut in half
- Seed beads, size 6°
    - 20 shiny green
    - 7 matte green
    - 16 shiny pink
    - 3 metallic pink
- Seed beads, size 8°
    - 17 metallic pink
    - 6 light pink
    - 11 light pink opaque
    - 11 matte black
    - 12 shiny pink
- Chain stabilization tool, optional
- Ear wires, set with crystals

HOW TO MAKE IT

Determine the shapes of the charms you want for your bracelet. Make small templates for any cookie cutter shapes you don't have, such as a cupcake. Roll out the metal clay 3 cards thick. Cut out various charm shapes using the cookie cutters and any templates you made. (The bracelet pictured features three leaves, two hearts, two flowers, two cupcakes, and a dragonfly.) Cut out two extra cupcakes for the earrings. Cut out a large circle for the bracelet's center element and a leaf shape and a bar for the toggle clasp. Sculpt a small clay heart by hand. (Later, you will attach this heart to the large circle.)

cupcake charm bracelet with earrings

Use a craft knife to make a hole through the top of each charm. Use a pencil to draw designs onto the clay charms, and carve them out with a carving tool as shown in photo A. Create small indentations in the center of several charms to hold chatons. Let all clay parts dry.

Place the dry clay components on a kiln shelf. Following the kiln manufacturer's instructions, fire the clay. Tumble the fired charms until you're satisfied with the polish, but do not tumble the hand-sculpted heart and large circle. Make 12 equidistant marks near the edge and all the way around the fired clay circle. Punch a hole in the clay at each mark with the metal hole punch pliers (photo B).

Place a cupcake charm on the steel bench block. Use the chasing hammer and the heart stamp to make a random pattern on the cupcake charm (photo C). Repeat this process on the rest of the cupcake charms.

A

B

To add texture to the circle, place it on the steel bench block and tap it with the small end of the chasing hammer. Pound as much texture as desired. Repeat this process with the toggle and the toggle bar. Color everything with a black permanent marker, and then buff the surface with a polishing pad.

Mix the two-part epoxy, following the manufacturer's instructions. Use it to adhere the chatons and flat back crystals onto the charms; affix the sculpted heart to the center of the circle; and attach cup chain strands to the middle of the cupcake charms, as shown in photo D.

Feed five small jump rings and five large jump rings through the holes in the circle, alternating the ring sizes and adding three to four seed beads to each ring before closing it. Attach one section of black chain to each side jump ring on the circle.

TIP

Using a chain stabilizer to hold your bracelet taut while adding jump rings is a lifesaver!

Thread one seed bead, a charm, and a second seed bead on each twist jump ring. Thread from three to five seeds beads in a random but pleasing order on 12 large jump rings.

Attach and alternate a jump ring with seed beads and a charm with seed beads to both sections of the chain, making sure to set aside two cupcake charms for the earrings. Attach the leaf shaped toggle to one end of the chain with a jump ring. Attach the bar to the other end of the chain.

Feed an ear wire set with crystals through the hole at the top of each of the two extra cupcake charms.

C

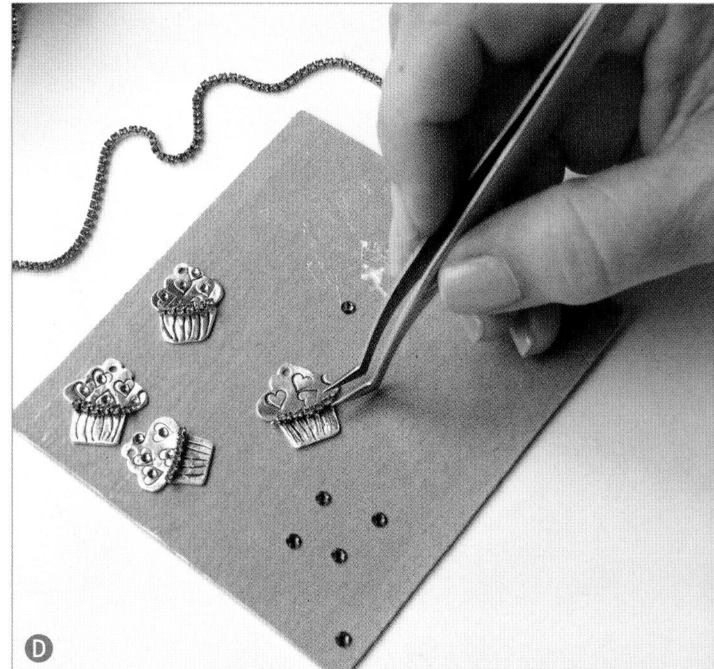
D

idea book

Jackie Truty
Fuchsia Bouquet

Jackie Truty
Into the Garden

Janet Alexander
Ring Around the Rosie

Cindy Thomas Pankopf
Bamboo Toggle

Lorena Angulo
Roses

Kristal Wick
Bling Ring

Kristal Wick
Silk and Sterling

Cindy Thomas Pankopf
Fuchsia Pendant

Jackie Truty
Amber Harvest

Janet Alexander
Star Gazer

Janet Alexander
Atlantis Risen

Lorena Angulo
Penacho Arbol De Vida

Cindy Thomas Pankopf
Magnetic Focal Clasp

Christina Orlikowski and Kristal Wick
Copper Heart Necklace

Lorena Angulo
Goddess Coatlicue

Cindy Thomas Pankopf
Anthurium Trio

acknowledgments

Thanks to the folks at Lark Books and Sterling Publishing for everything! I am honored to be one of your authors.

To Ray Hemachandra for turning this idea into reality.

To Kathy Sheldon for her blood, sweat, and humor.

To Leslie Rogalski and Melinda Barta who turned me into a seed-beadaholic!

To my adorable muses, Sparkle and Bling.

Special thanks to Chris Orlikowski for talking me off the creative cliff more than once, her boundless talent, and her endless friendship.

A special thanks to my fave companies who donated the goodies for this book: Swarovski Elements; Tierra Cast; Vintaj; ArtBeads; Beadalon; Ala Carte Clasp and WireLace; Bead Trust; Kabella Design, Clear Snap; Plaid; Susan Lenart Kazmer; Garlan Chain; Ogilvie, Inc.; CJS Sales Ltd.; Dreamtime Creations, Bead Stopper, and Ranger.

about the author

Residing in Colorado, international award-winning designer and Swarovski ambassador Kristal Wick has been represented in galleries spanning the globe, including Canyon Road in Santa Fe, New Mexico; Alaska; the Cayman Islands, Italy; Germany; and the Virgin Islands.

Previously the editor of BeadingDaily.com, Kristal is the author of *Foxy Epoxy*, *Sassy Silky Savvy*, and *Fabulous Fabric Beads* (a best seller in five categories on Amazon.com). Kristal also has two DVDs, *Mixed Media: Beaded Bracelets with Fiber Beads, Crystals, Resin, and Wire* and *Mixed Media: Jewelry Making with Handmade Beads, Crystals, Resin, and More!*

A jewelry design expert and blogger, Kristal teaches worldwide at quilt and bead shows and on cruise ships. She has created jewelry for the Jimmy Buffet Band, Ali McGraw, and Marianne Williamson. She is a frequent guest on HGTV and PBS, and her designs have been featured in more than 45 publications including: *Belle Armoire, Vogue Patterns, Lapidary Journal, Stringing, Beadwork, Bead Style, Crafts Business, Simply Beads, SewNews, Sewing Savvy, Piecework, Step by Step Beads, Crafts Report, Crafts-n-Things*, and *Bead Design Studio*.

Kristal is available for book signings, workshops, lectures, trunk shows, and freelance design. Sign up for her free online newsletter at KristalWick.com.

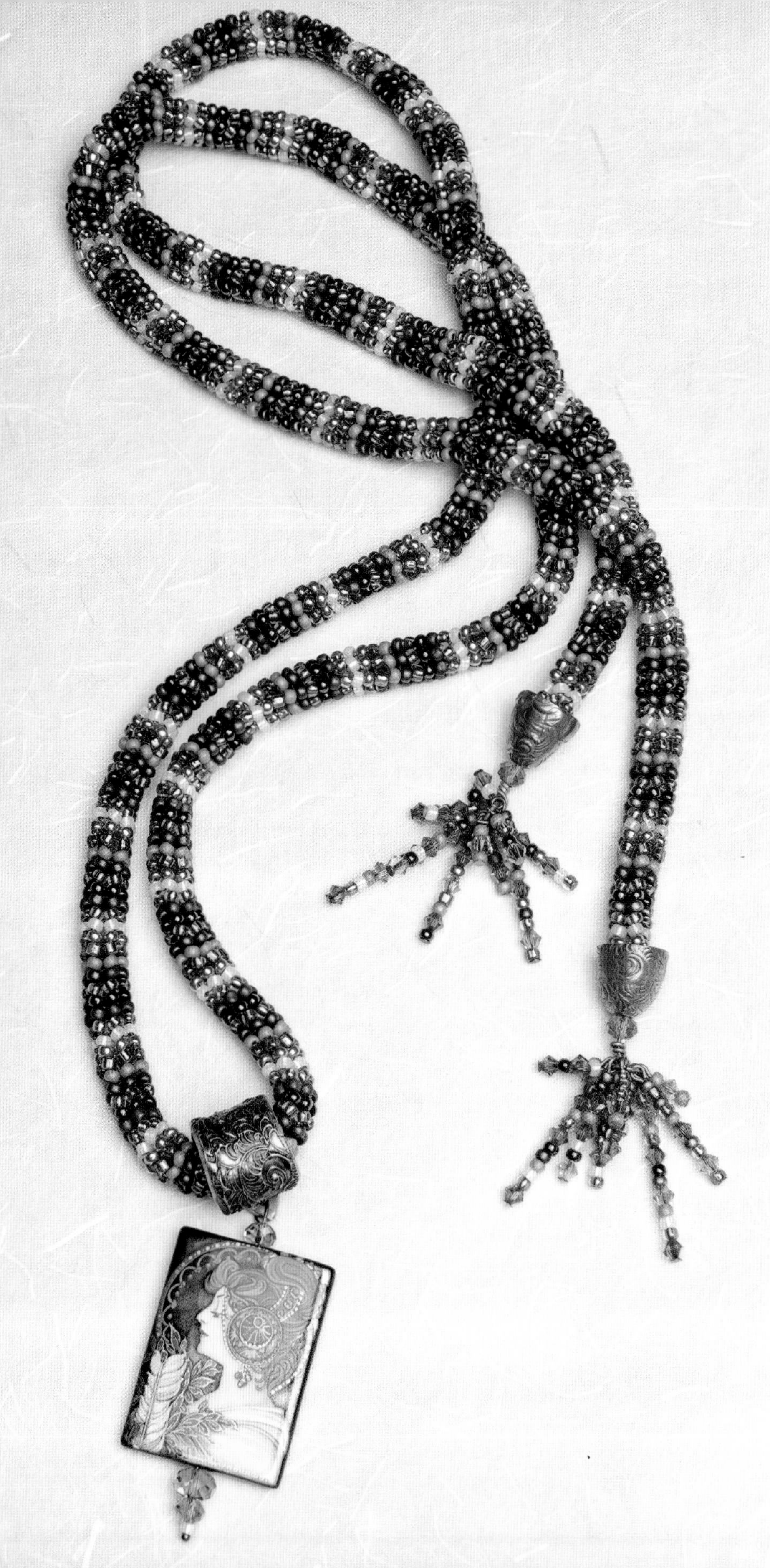

credits

EDITOR
Kathy Sheldon

ART DIRECTOR
Kay Holmes Stafford

EDITORIAL ASSISTANCE
Dawn Dillingham

PHOTOGRAPHERS
Lynne Harty
Christine Orlikowski

COVER DESIGNER
Kay Holmes Stafford

index